Help for the
Post Abortion
Woman

Help for the Post Abortion Woman

Teri Reisser, M.S.
and
Paul Reisser, M.D.

LIFE CYCLE BOOKS LTD.
Toronto, Ontario • Lewiston, New York

Published by: *U.S.A. Office*
Life Cycle Books Ltd.   Life Cycle Books
2205 Danforth Ave   PO Box 420
Toronto, ON M4C 1K4   Lewiston, NY 14092-0420

Printed and bound in Canada

ISBN 0-919225-44-6

Contents

Foreword

I nduced abortion has been legal in this country for more than twenty-one years. During that time period, the irrevocable abortion decision has been made over thirty million times. While the media and most professional mental health organizations have declared abortion to be psychologically safe, abundant research and clinical evidence suggest otherwise. I know this all too well, having interviewed and treated since 1973 hundreds of women and men who have been emotionally harmed by their abortion experience.

Typically, these individuals shoulder the aftermath of their decision in silence: shamed, guilt-ridden, depressed and–most importantly–alone. Much research affirms the reluctance of women to acknowledge their abortion in general, and their unspoken grief in particular. The price of unacknowledged and unresolved abortion grief is great. Far too many women and men live shattered lives for fear of facing this unspeakable loss–the intentional death of their own child.

When our culture minimizes and/or denies the psychological after-effects of abortion, and when individuals are made to feel deviant if they acknowledge post-abortion grief, how can one heal, and where can one turn for help? Teri and Paul Reisser's book, *Help for the Post-abortion Woman* is an important and sensitive first step. Because there are so few books written on this topic, the Reissers' contribution is especially welcome and necessary.

This book is for women and men in pain. It is genuine, compassionate and practical. It also speaks the truth about the emotional traumatization so many have experienced after abortion, a rarely told story that desperately needs to be shared. The Reissers' experience in caring for women and men emotionally scarred from abortion is similar to my own at the Institute for Pregnancy Loss in New Hampshire, as well as that of other attentive clinicians both in this country and abroad. The trauma-based stories of these individuals are all similar, and yet uniquely different.

Help for the Post-abortion Woman is for women and men who seek recovery and wholeness. It is not always easy reading, since the tasks of grief work and emotional resolution are never effortless. But throughout this book, the reader is clearly guided through an understanding of post-abortion trauma and the steps necessary to begin healing.

This small book makes a significant contribution, presenting a great deal of information in a very readable manner. I would encourage the reader who has been involved in one or more abortion decisions to be unafraid of seeking greater understanding of the unwelcome feelings and perceptions they have experienced subsequently. This book can genuinely help those who sense that something isn't right within, but do not understand their feelings. As caregivers, the Reissers are well-experienced with the complexity of bereavement, and possess the gentleness of heart and word so necessary to encourage recovery.

> Vincent M. Rue, Ph.D.
> Co-Director
> Institute for Pregnancy Loss
> Portsmouth, New Hampshire.

Preface

*I*n 1985 we took an active part in the formation of a Crisis Pregnancy Center (CPC) in our community. Like hundreds of other CPCs in the United States, our local center is a labor of love designed to support alternatives to abortion for women whose pregnancies are, for any number of reasons, a major problem in their lives. Before the center opened, and during its early months of operation, Teri was approached by several women who wanted to talk about past abortions, not current pregnancies. Their comments were quite surprising.

All of these women appeared to be functioning well in their everyday lives. Yet as they told their stories (usually about abortions which had occurred years before) they would express intense emotion, often stopping for several minutes of quiet weeping. Most of them stated that they had never described their experiences to anyone, and a few even realized that they had completely suppressed the memory of another abortion.

None of these women had been solicited to tell their story, nor had they recently been whipped into a frenzy at an emotional pro-life rally. Furthermore, there were no horror stories about back-alley procedures. Most of the abortions had been perfectly legal, and were carried out by competent physicians. The women were simply carrying a very deep pain, which had been walled-off like a dormant infection but which also at times influenced other areas of their lives.

Teri was both fascinated and deeply moved by these encounters. Since she was in the midst of earning a graduate degree in counseling, she decided to check the professional literature for additional information about emotional problems following abortion. What she found was equally fascinating: a computer search of thousands of psychological journal articles written over the past several years yielded only fourteen references on this subject.[1] These articles, and many of the books on abortion written for the general public, offered the same conclusion: any kind of significant emotional reaction following abortion was extremely rare. Some women might have a short case of "the blues" afterwards, but this could be explained by changes in hormone levels after the pregnancy ended.

Over the following several months, hundreds of encounters with women who were experiencing pain in the wake of abortion led to a strikingly different conclusion: psychological and spiritual suffering following abortion is not at all uncommon, and hormonal changes or "the blues" are a woefully inadequate explanation for a disturbance which may continue for many years. A number of researchers and therapists nationwide have observed similar patterns, leading to the coining of the term "Post Abortion Syndrome" (PAS).

Many conferences and workshops have subsequently served to clarify the dimensions of Post Abortion Syndrome, and have led to the development of approaches to recovery. Over the years, Teri has had the opportunity to conduct a number of seminars on this subject, some under the auspices of the Post Abortion Counseling and Education (or PACE) program of the Christian Action Council (since renamed CareNet). This book contains much of the seminar material, and is written for two audiences: first, for women who are (or think they may be) suffering in the wake of abortion, and second for those who desire, as counselors or loving friends, to understand and help women with Post Abortion Syndrome.

One brief note on terminology: throughout this book we will frequently use the terms "pro-life" and "pro-choice" to refer to the opposing forces in the ongoing abortion controversy. Although each term encompasses a spectrum of opinion, we will assume that "pro-life" refers to the position that the fetus is a human being entitled to legal protection and that abortion is therefore inherently wrong, and that "pro-choice" designates the viewpoint that a pregnant woman has the ultimate right to decide, on whatever basis, whether or not to continue her pregnancy.

We want to express our loving thanks to Chad and Carrie, who displayed maturity beyond their years while mom and dad worked on this important project.

We are also indebted to the counselors whose work is reflected in these pages: Linda Ross, Linda Cochrane, Cathy Barnard, Vincent Rue, Anne Speckhard, and Penny Salazar.

And most importantly, the greatest gratitude goes to the women who experienced healing in the post abortion groups. Their recovery processes were the building blocks of this book. It is our prayer that their stories will touch the reader and give her hope.

---

1. Since 1985, many more articles have been written on the emotional aftermath of abortion.

Chapter 1:
One Woman's Story

*L*inda's seventeenth birthday was a typical school day. Like the previous 365 days of her life, it came and went without incident. Classes (which had rudely brought summer to a halt only a week before) proceeded in an orderly sequence. Lunch offered the usual uninspired fare, hot gossip was in short supply, and nothing resembling romance was on the horizon.

This day, like her life, was just average. Actually, there was a brief but pleasurable distraction after school, as a few of her friends treated her to frozen yogurt at the mall. No big deal, they said, but it meant a lot to her. As she watched them rustle through cluttered purses in search of loose change, and listened to their noisy efforts to figure out who had the hots for whom, Linda was struck by how much she was like them: neither rich nor broke, neither brilliant nor dumb, neither gorgeous nor ugly. Similar homes, similar neighborhoods, similar families—indeed, their common ground included the fact that nearly everyone's parents, including hers, had been divorced.

For Linda, this event had come at the worst possible time, during an eighth grade semester which felt like four months of fingers on the chalkboard. The muffled sounds of her mom and dad fighting late at night turned Linda's stomach inside out, and their separation didn't provide much relief. Her dad settled into a condo and a new relationship not long after the ink had dried on the legal papers, and Linda spent every other weekend with him in a futile effort to stay close. By her seventeenth birthday, her visits came every other month. Linda's mom tried to keep the house and her wounds in reasonable condition, and the two of them managed to have some good times together as Linda emerged from the uncivilized world of junior high school. But eventually Linda started dating.

Perhaps Linda's mom was still smarting from her husband's sudden departure for greener (and younger) pastures. Maybe she had spent too many years worrying about her little girl's entry into womanhood. Or could it be that she had a few high school secrets of her own? Whatever the cause, Linda was dismayed by her mom's scrutiny of every member of the opposite sex who came within a block of the front door. Even the simplest date seemed to produce a congressional investigation the next morning. And the going got tougher after Linda met Steven. He was polite, quite intelligent, and above all attentive to Linda in ways no one had been before. Within a few weeks the shallow rituals of dating gave way to long talks, deep emotion and the inevitable desire for intimacy. As her dream of married life with Steven after graduation became more focused, Linda's old list of do's and don'ts slowly faded from memory. Their relationship intensified, and so did Mom's continual lectures about getting "too serious" with him. But Linda held her ground.

On the first day of spring break, Linda drove several miles to a drugstore in another community, made a purchase, and then slipped into the ladies' room of a nearby coffee shop. She read and reread the directions on the test she had bought, then watched with horror as it quietly informed her that she was pregnant. How could this have happened when they had been so careful?

She called Steven, who drove over immediately and met her with support, reassurance and a very specific resolve. He was surprisingly calm, as if he had expected this conversation and rehearsed his lines. While she stared at her soft drink and fiddled with the pregnancy test, he spelled out his conclusion that an abortion would be the only sensible solution to their problem. He would even pay for it. But somewhere in the distant past Linda had concluded that abortion was wrong. Now, for the first time, she said so. Thus began their very first serious fight.

Unfortunately, the alternatives to abortion appeared dismal, and Steven wasted no time painting several gloomy pictures. How would her mom react after all the big lectures about "going too far"? She would probably try to ground Linda for the next decade, and life without Steven would be unbearable. What about her dad? He was so wrapped up with his new wife and her two kids that he wanted little more than an occasional phone call from Linda informing him that his own little girl was "just fine." A problem like this would kill him, if he didn't kill her (or Steven) first. And how about college? Who wants to have a baby in the middle of her freshman year? Who would pay the bills? The idea of changing diapers in the middle of a cram session for midterms sounded ridiculous.

The argument ended in a lopsided stalemate as Linda held her ground about the abortion. She realized, though, that Steven was probably right. She was being too emotional about this decision, and not thinking logically. Still, when they parted that afternoon, their embrace lacked its usual intensity. The powerful feeling of comfort and abandon Linda usually felt in Steven's arms had changed. It would never be the same again.

Only two of Linda's most trusted friends heard about the pregnancy and the fight, and both said without a moment's hesitation that even considering having the baby was crazy. All of her hopes and plans with Steven would have to be seriously revised. And, they predicted, Steven would probably start looking elsewhere once Linda's bikini refused to fit. So, before spring break ended, she agreed to let Steven schedule the abortion.

On the appointed day, Linda and Steven drove across town to a women's health center. The receptionist was friendly, brisk and efficient, and a counselor assured her that the procedure was no worse than having a wisdom tooth extracted. When she began to express some doubts, she was reminded that only she could make the decision, and that her doubts weren't all that unusual. Did she want to go home and think it over? Linda quickly replayed the argument with Steven and the gloomy scenarios of a pregnancy turning her life upside down. No, she sighed, let's get this over with. The counselor affirmed her decision, and assured her she would be just fine.

When she returned to the waiting room, Linda was amazed by the low-key atmosphere. Some women were chatting with one another as though they were waiting for a bus, while others leafed through fashion magazines. No one entering or leaving the clinic seemed to be upset. The counselor was probably right—she would be just fine.

Linda maintained control through the bored greeting by a doctor who forgot to introduce himself, the sting of the anesthetic, the cramping, the suction noises, the sound of something going through a plastic tube. But when it was all over, she wept inconsolably, as if grieving a terrible loss. The nurse wasn't much help as Linda sobbed quietly in the recovery area. There just wasn't enough time to hold anyone's hand on a busy morning like this.

On the drive home, Steven couldn't think of much to say. He was very attentive for a few days but eventually became irritated by her mood swings. Gradually a coolness crept into their relationship, and when Steven finally suggested that they break up she felt surprisingly indifferent. By the time graduation day arrived, Linda had stopped thinking about Steven, wedding plans, or the abortion.

Linda spent the next four years immersed in college life. She studied hard and dated a lot, being careful not to develop emotional ties to anyone in particular, and never forgetting to take her birth control pills. Like a scar, the combination of a busy schedule and a sense of numbness protected her from feeling anything too deeply. But two years after graduation she met John, who seemed to ride into her life like Prince Charming. He was adept at handling all the surface banter Linda had cultivated during college, but before long he broke through it and resurrected feelings she had avoided for years. A flurry of dates led to an engagement ring presented with great finesse during a candlelight dinner, and a wedding six months later.

As their first anniversary approached, John began talking about starting a family. Not much had been said about this during the preceding months, and now for some reason John's most casual comments about little people running around the house set off a quiet panic inside of Linda. She avoided this topic as much as possible, but eventually a few romantic evenings and John's smoothest talk over wine and fresh flowers proved irresistible. What could be better than to raise children with such a wonderful husband?

Yet as they officially trashed her birth control pills in an impromptu ceremony, a growing depression began to crowd in on Linda like a gathering storm. She manufactured reasons to avoid sex, especially midway through her cycle. She found herself awakening, cold and covered with sweat, in the middle of the night, trying to remember the details of nightmares which seemed to have something to do with babies or lost children.

When John's sister and her husband arrived for a weekend to show off their newborn daughter, Linda could barely make conversation. After this awkward visit ended, she began thinking about the baby she had aborted. With her thoughts came tears, like an uncontrolled flood, at odd hours of the day. Even a Pampers commercial would provoke a hasty departure to the bathroom in search of Kleenex.

Increasingly concerned about his wife's moods, John managed one night to convince Linda to talk about what was bothering her. She had kept her abortion a secret from him until now, and he did an admirable job listening to her story without showing much reaction. But afterwards his nightly jogging session became a feverish sprint as wretched images tore through his mind again and again. He knew Linda had not been inexperienced when they met (nor had he), but somehow this procedure, though now only a memory, had become an ugly and powerful intruder in their marriage. There was no way they could work past this pain without some help.

During Linda's first session with the marriage counselor she was encouraged to ventilate her feelings toward those involved in the abortion experience. A venomous blast against her parents and her old boyfriend surprised Linda and impressed the therapist. The experience was cathartic, and she went home feeling better than she had in months. But before three days had passed she had plummeted to a new level of depression.

At the next session the therapist suggested that they needed to leave the abortion episode behind and focus on her present relationships. When Linda brought up the abortion again the following week, the counselor assured her that a past abortion could not be the cause of a serious depression. They had other work to do, and she could not continue dwelling on this single episode as an excuse for her present condition. In addition, the counselor recommended that she might be a candidate for anti-depressant medication, and arranged for a brief psychiatric consultation to explore this option.

After another month of tears, fitful sleep and a dry mouth from her new medication, Linda felt confused and discouraged. As she lay next to John on a muggy Thursday night, all she could think about was what a colossal mess she had made of her life. *Why bother with the endless, expensive therapy sessions? John is spending so much on a problem he had nothing to do with—maybe he'd be better off without me. And who needs this drug and all its lousy side effects? I think I'll flush them down the toilet. On second, thought, maybe I should just take them all at once...*

Chapter 2:
How Do I Know
If I Need This Book?

L inda's story in the previous chapter is a composite of several women's experiences, and although the names and some other identifying elements have been changed (as they will in other stories throughout this book), the events are true. They are also by no means unique.

This year thousands of "Lindas" will become pregnant when they least want or expect to be. They will agonize over their pregnancy and their circumstances—perhaps by themselves, but more often with the baby's father, or their girlfriends, or perhaps their parents. They will decide to have an abortion, but with very mixed feelings. They will feel some relief at first, but months (or more often years) later will begin experiencing emotional pain which may become disabling. And they may consult a counselor or therapist who does not recognize, or will trivialize, the role one or more past abortions is playing in the current emotional turmoil.

Perhaps, in one or more ways, you are like Linda. You may be convinced that (or wondering if) the depression, or anxiety, or nightmares, or any of a dozen other symptoms are related to an abortion in your past. You may have scanned the titles of multitudes of self-help books in your local mall, looking for one which would at least confirm that a past abortion might continue to cause problems, even years after the procedure.

Perhaps you have never told your "secret" to anyone else, because you feared their reaction. Yet with one out of four pregnancies in America ending in abortion for a generation of women, it is likely that one or more women you know share the same secret. Many who appear calm and competent on the surface may be struggling with the same issues, but afraid to bring them up. After all, even women who firmly believe in the right to have an abortion rarely relish talking about their own. This is not a likely topic for the dinner table, or conversation over the back fence, or the Wednesday night prayer meeting, or even a close support group.

If you have had an abortion within the past several weeks and have been in acute emotional pain ever since, your inability to deny the conflict you feel may work in your favor—if you address that pain NOW. By doing so, you will save yourself years of disruption caused by driving that pain into the uncharted depths of your subconscious. Unfortunately, the majority of women who have experienced distress shortly after an abortion endure years of unhealthy relationships and living patterns before coming to the point where they finally deal with the pain.

If you are many years from your abortion experience, you may feel as if you have two competing voices inside you—one that keeps insisting that you are doing just fine with the abortion, and another that reminds you that your conflict has never been settled. If you have recently started thinking about it again, it is probably time to give the second voice a chance to be heard. Listening to it may seem a terrifying proposition, but the longer you refuse to listen the harder it will be to face and deal with the painful memories you cannot forever keep repressed.

Here are some key questions to ask yourself.[1] Be honest and pay attention to any emotional or physical reactions you may have to particular questions These will give you some important clues as to whether you need healing from a previous abortion:

- Do you find yourself struggling to turn off feelings connected to your abortion(s), perhaps telling yourself over and over again to forget about it?

- Do you find yourself avoiding books, magazines and television programs that deal with the subject of abortion?

- Are you affected by physical reminders of your abortion (babies, pregnant women, etc.)?

- Are you uncomfortable around children?

- Are there certain times of the year you find yourself depressed, sick or accident prone—especially around the anniversary date of the abortion or the would-be birth date?

- Are you resentful and unforgiving towards anyone because of his or her involvement in your abortion(s)—parents, boyfriend, abortionist, friends, or husband?

- Are you in a situation where you could find yourself faced with another unwanted pregnancy?

- Do you have trouble with emotional intimacy since your abortion?

- Have you experienced periods of prolonged depression since your abortion? Have you had any suicidal thoughts?

- Have you experienced any peculiar occurrences relating to the abortion experience, such as nightmares about babies, flashbacks, or hallucinations (for example, hearing a baby cry)?

- Are you able to talk about abortion? When choosing to share about your abortion(s), are you overcome with strong feelings?

- If you have children now, do you smother them with your love or overprotect them? Are you unable to bond with the children you now have?

- If you do not have children, do you fear that you will never be able to have them (either because of physical harm resulting from the abortion or because God won't allow you)?

- Do you tend to look at your life in terms of "before" and "after" the abortion(s)? Has your self-concept changed?

- Have you found yourself preoccupied with thoughts of your aborted child lately?

- Did your relationship to or concept of God change after your abortion? How?

If you answered yes to one or more of the above questions, and especially if you had an emotional or physical response to any of them, you are probably suffering from a problem known as Post Abortion Syndrome. You will most likely benefit from exploring the contents of this book.

We hope that the information offered in the following chapters will help you understand what happened to you emotionally during and after the time of your abortion decision, and (more importantly) help you experience healing for the guilt, anger and/or grief you may feel.

---

1. Most of these questions are taken from the excellent post abortion workbook, *Women In Ramah*, authored by a dear friend and gifted woman, Linda Cochrane. (See bibliography for ordering information.)

Chapter 3:
The Silent Epidemic

M any of us remember the late 1960s and early 1970s as a time of widespread sit-ins and marches protesting America's involvement in the Vietnam war. At the same time, a smaller movement was intensely protesting American's abortion laws. Before the Supreme Court wrote its landmark *Roe v. Wade* decision of 1973, the majority of states either restricted or completely outlawed abortion. Individuals and groups working to legalize abortion (such as the National Association for the Repeal of Abortion Laws—NARAL[1]) argued vigorously that women carrying unwanted pregnancies were inevitably traumatized in two ways.

First, they claimed that women who were forced to deliver babies they didn't want often suffered great emotional distress. In fact, prior to 1973 a number of states allowed a woman to abort if a psychiatrist would attest that severe psychological harm would occur if the pregnancy continued. In some cities, pro-abortion therapists were more than willing to escort women quickly through this requirement, without a detailed evaluation. This argument made a very important assumption: if denying an abortion to a woman who desperately wanted one was harmful to her, then providing an abortion for her would lead to psychological well-being.

The other pre-1973 argument for legalizing abortion is still raised automatically today whenever any restriction on abortion is proposed. Women who were desperate to end their pregnancies would subject themselves to the harrowing world of the "back-alley" abortionist. Those who survived the incompetent medical care often told horror stories of searing pain, humiliation and overt sexual harassment by their "doctor." There was (and is) no question that these experiences scarred thousands of women, physically and emotionally. In contrast to such disasters, the idea of a legal abortion carried out by a well-trained physician, in a clinic staffed by supportive counselors and nurses, seemed like a heavenly vision.

Thus, when abortion suddenly became readily available in 1973, few stopped to ponder whether legal and relatively safe abortions might cause significant problems. Since that time, a vocal contingent of speakers, authors and professionals has continued to insist that abortion has no important emotional consequences, unless a woman is already unbalanced. Consider the following examples:

In a 1988 radio debate with Teri, the medical director of Planned Parenthood in Los Angeles flatly stated that only a hundred or so women every year (out of 1.5 million who have abortions nationwide) experience any significant emotional distress in the wake of this procedure. It is unlikely, of course, that a major abortion provider would be inclined to sound a warning about its own service, but this figure represents an astonishing confidence on Planned Parenthood's part that so little could go wrong. In the three years prior to this radio talk show, drawing from our own community of 100,000, Teri alone had worked in depth with well over 100 women who had experienced major difficulties in the wake of a past abortion decision. (These women sought counseling on their own initiative, based on a yellow pages ad for the Crisis Pregnancy Center which included "Post-Abortion Counseling".)

Many books written for the general public are more blunt in their conviction that having an abortion shouldn't give anyone much grief. A popular collection of health information for women is *The New Our Bodies, Ourselves*, a 1984 revision of the best-selling *Our Bodies, Ourselves*. In a section entitled "Feelings After an Abortion," the authors state,

> Severe depression after an abortion is extremely rare. In fact, it is much less likely than severe depression after childbirth. A few women experience feelings of sadness or depression years later at around the time of year when they had the abortion or when they would have given birth.

> Women sometimes feel guilty, which is understandable in a society that doesn't particularly accept the choice of abortion. So much emphasis is put on motherhood that many people act as though a fetus is more important than a woman...

> If you were not able to work through your feelings before the abortion, you may feel troubled afterwards. Being able to talk about your feelings with a sympathetic and objective friend, relative, counselor or group is the most important thing you can do to help you feel better, resolve difficulties and move on.[2]

Another book, *The Abortion Controversy*, discusses abortion procedures, the *Roe v. Wade* decision and its aftermath, and the two sides of the issue in rather plain language geared for a teenage audience. In a section entitled "The Psychological Effects," author Carol Emmons states somewhat blandly,

> An abortion can sometimes cause emotional or psychological problems. They are generally considered minor upsets, however.

According to the Institute of Medicine of the National Academy of Sciences, there is no evidence of serious mental illness caused by having an abortion.[3]

She continues by mentioning briefly some reasons why guilt may occur after abortion, but then concludes with the statement:

It is worth noting that more women are depressed following childbirth than following an abortion. After childbirth, many women have the "baby blues," or postpartum depression. In part, this feeling is caused by hormonal changes in the body.[4]

The role of hormones in post-abortion emotions is a common theme in other books written for lay audiences. Beryl Lieff Benderly, in her book *Thinking About Abortion*, writes:

But what about the emotions, which have played such a vital part in the woman's experience? This answer often involves ... the hormones. ... Although many women feel relief as their overriding, immediate and lasting reaction, many also report "the blues," "the dumps," or a "funk" for the next few days. This usually isn't a serious depression but rather the same "down" feeling that plagues many women every month with their periods or right after they deliver a baby. And it comes from the same cause: hormone swings often mean mood swings as well.[5]

This explanation, of course, offers little insight into any prolonged or delayed feelings of guilt or despair which a woman might experience. Authors

Maria Corsaro and Carole Korzeniowski, in *A Woman's Guide to Safe Abortion*, elaborate on the hormonal situation and add a few additional reasons why one might feel unhappy after an abortion:

> Many women feel slightly "down" after the abortion. This may be connected with the hormonal change. If you've felt this sort of thing before, during your monthly ovulation or menstruation, then you know what we mean. Added to that, of course, is the strain of rushing around to arrange for tests and the abortion, and the physical stress of the operation itself. So if you feel a little weepy and shaky, it's very understandable...
>
> If you're having any of these feelings after the abortion, it can help to know that many women feel the same way. A few tears and a tinge of the blues is perfectly normal in the first few days.[6]

A similar viewpoint prevails in the books and journal articles written by and for physicians and psychologists. For example, the current edition of a standard, widely distributed psychiatry textbook devotes most of its section on abortion to the stress of carrying an unwanted pregnancy.[7] This would seem to be an odd subject to cover at a time when abortion is so readily available, but it reveals a notion expressed in much of the professional literature: the problems caused by abortions are trivial compared to those brought by having a child under stressful (or even ideal) circumstances.[8]

More recently, in January, 1989 the American Psychological Association (APA) stated that its survey of the current professional literature indicated that most women do not suffer lasting effects from abortion. Brian Wilcox, Director of Public Interest Legislation for the APA, stated, "It's clear that the vast majority of women are not going to experience any significant problems. Millions of women are having abortions, and it appears to be a relatively benign procedure both medically and psychologically."[9] Yet as impressive as this statement and others like it sound, they simply do not tell the whole story. Over the past few years there has arisen a serious challenge to the notion that abortion is a "relatively benign procedure."

In 1982, Nancyjo Mann established a group called Women Exploited By Abortion (WEBA). Her goal was to offer support and a voice for women who, like herself, felt they had been damaged by a past abortion. As Ms. Mann appeared on radio and television interviews, thousands of women discovered that they were not alone in their pain. Many literally came out of the closet in order to join WEBA support groups, which today are meeting in every state of the country.

In scattered locations throughout the United States, a few therapists began seriously listening to women who were reporting pain after their abortions. As they located one another and compared notes, they noticed striking similarities in their post-abortion clients. There appeared to be much more to this issue than a few unbalanced women whining about their abortions. There were instead thousands, perhaps millions, of women for whom abortion had not spelled "relief," but rather heartache and even despair.

Pioneer researchers, such as Drs. Anne Speckhard, Vincent Rue, Arthur Shostack and David Reardon, began organizing and publishing their findings, eventually coining the term "post abortion syndrome" (or PAS) to describe the condition they saw repeatedly. Most investigators in this new field came to agree with Anne Speckhard's definition of PAS: a person's inability to: (1) process the fear, anger, sadness and guilt surrounding her abortion experience, (2) grieve (or even name) the loss of the baby, and (3) come to peace with God, her- or himself and others involved in the abortion decision. (Most therapists in this field acknowledge that any person involved in the abortion decision is a possible candidate for PAS.)

They also took a hard look at the journal articles which had concluded that few women were troubled following abortion, and found some serious weaknesses in the way these studies were written.[10] Meanwhile, books detailing individual post-abortion experiences of pain and subsequent healing began to appear on the market for the general public. (*Will I Cry Tomorrow?* by Susan Stanford, *Helping Women Recover From Abortion* by Nancy Michels, *Beyond Choice* by Don Baker, and *Abortion's Second Victim* by Pam Koerbel are examples.)

Concern over the effects of abortion on women eventually reached the highest levels of government. In 1987 President Reagan ordered Surgeon General C. Everett Koop to review the medical and psychological risks of abortion, and report his findings to the public. In January, 1989 Dr. Koop concluded only that he could not draw sweeping conclusions from the scientific evidence currently available. Instead he urged that a large-scale, comprehensive study be organized, one that could take five years to complete and potentially cost 100 million dollars.

The bottom line is this: far too many women (and men) are suffering emotional pain resulting from an abortion to be ignored, even though scientific research has not yet fully defined the scope of the problem. No one knows how many women are affected, but there are good reasons to believe that the number extends into the hundreds of thousands.

There are deep and usually conflicting emotions involved in nearly every abortion decision. To consider an abortion to be a trivial event in a woman's life (equivalent to having a wisdom tooth extracted, as too many abortion clinics suggest) is naive indeed. A sizable number of women enter clinics and hospitals believing that abortion is wrong but convinced that they have no other reasonable choice. One 1981 opinion poll of 1,105 women, compiled in part by a sociologist from Planned Parenthood's own research organization, found that 24% of women who had had abortions considered the procedure morally wrong.[11] Assuming that this percentage is still accurate, at least one out of four women having an abortion (over 375,000 every year) is violating her own moral standards. (This, in fact, is one of the most common issues reported by women who seek help months or years after an abortion.)

Another article written for *Feminist Perspectives on Social Work and Human Sexuality* admitted that "The proportion of women who experience varying degrees of post-abortion stress ranges from less than 10% for possible psychiatric sequelae to 50% for feelings of unhappiness or troubled thoughts...it is superfluous to ask whether patients experience guilt—it is axiomatic that they will".[12]

Overall, the problem involves more than statistics and journal articles. There are thousands of individuals who have been deeply affected by abortion and who need healing. As post abortion syndrome has been more widely discussed and debated in the media, more women (as well as men, siblings, and grandparents) are coming forward to find the help they so badly need. In lecturing across the country on the subject, Teri has had conversations with hundreds of post-abortion women who were willing to travel long distances to seek help, and who have been bewildered by the ignorance of local therapists on this issue.

The tide is finally turning. More and more post-abortion women are watching public television shows on prenatal development. And as they watch in wonder as their later, "planned" 10-week-old baby swims actively in utero during a routine sonagram, they begin to understand the grand deception that has been played on them by those in the feminist movement who assured them it was "nothing but a couple of tablespoons of blood".

For those who now realizing that they may need help, or who know someone who does, it is important to understand the symptoms which can occur sooner or later after an abortion — what they are, and how they start.

1. This organization later changed its name to the National Abortion Rights Action League.
2. The Boston Women's Health Collective, Ed., *The New Our Bodies, Ourselves* (New York: Simon and Schuster, 1984), p. 307.
3. Carol A. Emmons, *The Abortion Controversy* (New York: Julian Messner, 1987), p. 18.
4. Ibid., p. 21.
5. Beryl Lieff Benderly, *Thinking About Abortion* (Garden City, N.Y.: The Dial Press, 1984), p. 131.
6. Maria Corsaro and Carole Korzeniowsky, *A Woman's Guide to Safe Abortion* (New York: Holt, Rinehart and Winston, 1983), pp. 47, 58.
7. Judith E. Belsky, M.D., Livia S. Wan, M.D., and Gordon W. Douglas, M.D., "Abortion," in Harold I. Kaplan, M.D. and Benjamin J. Sadock, M.D., Eds., *Comprehensive Textbook of Psychiatry* (Baltimore: Williams and Witkins, 1985), pp. 1052-56.
8. Similarly, medical textbooks which list the possible physical complications of abortion inevitably add a comment that, statistically, abortion is safer than normal childbirth. This is, of course, useless information, not unlike saying that it is statistically safer to stay in the house than to go outside. Staying indoors may be safer, but very few of us take this into consideration when we need groceries. Likewise, even if abortion is statistically safer than childbirth, only a fool would propose that all pregnancies be terminated.
9. "Study: Abortion Harm Doesn't Last," *News Chronicle*, 25 January 1989, sec.1, p. 11.

10. The details of their work are too involved to review in this book. In essence, they have found weaknesses in the methods of collecting information from women following their abortion, as well as examples of bias in the interpretation of data.

11. The study was conducted by Greg Martire of the opinion research corporation Yankelovich, Skelly and White, and by Stanley K. Henshaw of the Alan Guttmacher Institute, the research arm of Planned Parenthood. Reported in "Abortion Clinics' Toughest Cases," *Medical World News*, March 9, 1987, p. 56.

12. Karen M. Lodl, Ann McGettigan, and Janette Bucy, "Women's Responses to Abortion: Implications for Post-Abortion Support Groups," *Feminist Perspectives on Social Work and Human Sexuality* (The Hawthorne Press, 1985).

Chapter 4:
How Post Abortion
Syndrome Develops

*I*n late 1986, American movie audiences were reintroduced to the Vietnam war in a new and powerful way. "Platoon" graphically portrayed the terror of combat from the foot-soldier's viewpoint, and tied enough stomachs in knots to win the Academy Award for Best Picture of the Year. Unfortunately, a number of viewers who had actually been in the war suffered more than a loss of appetite: they actually had emotional breakdowns during or after the movie. Why would this happen to people who had simply watched a film? The answer is important both to combat veterans and to many women who have experienced an abortion.

For more than a decade beginning in the late 1960s, psychologists working with soldiers who had served in Vietnam observed an alarming pattern. Men who had been previously well-adjusted were literally haunted by their experiences overseas. They could not rid themselves of recurring thoughts, images and dreams of the war. Many suffered disturbing symptoms such as sweating, pounding of the heart, and outbursts of anger or fear. Difficulty with relationships, and abuse of alcohol or drugs (an escape used by many during their tour of duty), was not unusual. A typical situation might involve a young veteran who would panic and dive for cover during a small-town fireworks show. And, more recently, many who walked into a showing of "Platoon" experienced a massive and disabling flashback, even though the war had been over for 12 years.

Therapists who worked with these men eventually described a syndrome which they called "Post Traumatic Stress Disorder" (PTSD). Because the Vietnam war had been such a politically and emotionally explosive issue in this country, the pioneer researchers found it difficult to convince many of their colleagues this disorder truly existed, and that many returning Vietnam veterans were its victims. (Indeed, 12 years elapsed before PTSD finally received formal recognition as a psychiatric diagnosis.)

Psychologists have since found that PTSD can affect anyone who has suffered through an intense and traumatic event which is not a part of normal experience—for example, close combat, a natural disaster (earthquake, flood, etc.), a serious accident, a violent incident such as torture or rape. All too often, victims of such episodes do not simply pick up with life where they left off. Instead, they undergo a variety of reactions which do not fade away with the passage of time. Many symptoms may not even become evident until years have passed. These typically include obsessive and intense memories of the event, a driving need to avoid anything which might bring it to mind, and a list of associated symptoms (including sleeping problems, eating and sexual disorders, depression, and so forth).

A number of therapists who have interviewed and counseled women with past abortions have noticed reaction patterns similar or identical to those we just listed. It appears, in fact, that Post Abortion Syndrome is a specific form of Post Traumatic Stress Disorder. Many of the details vary from case to case, and not all women experience a disturbing reaction in the months or years after an abortion. But for those who do (and we believe the number to be significant), there are some specific factors which can lead to this problem, and a common pattern of symptoms.

How Does Post Abortion Syndrome Develop?

For any form of Post Traumatic Stress Disorder to occur, there must be an event which is both traumatic and beyond the normal range of human experience. In the case of a war or disaster, the terror of the event is obvious. But abortion in the United States is legal and socially sanctioned, and over 4,000 occur every day. What would cause an abortion to be traumatic?

First of all, most women approach an abortion decision in a state of crisis. Discovering that one is pregnant is an emotionally charged moment, normally the cause either for great rejoicing or for terrible alarm. If the pregnancy represents a major problem, a woman will experience a tremendous amount of fear and anxiety, which will drive her either to seek a fast solution or to avoid dealing with it for as long as possible.

Eventually she must make some sort of decision—but it will be like few other decisions in life. It is likely to be affected by deeply rooted moral convictions, by strong opinions from family/boyfriend/husband, by mixed feelings about intimacy and sexuality, and by physical changes in her body. It may be discussed with a counselor or a close friend, but it won't be the subject of casual conversation. Thus, even though abortion is legal and to some degree socially sanctioned, and even though she may know someone who has had one, deciding to end a pregnancy still falls well outside the realm of most women's normal experience. It will remain her very uncomfortable secret, not a badge of honor.

Aside from the intensity of the decision to have an abortion, there are several other factors which may predispose a woman to emotional turmoil in the near or distant future:

1) **First and foremost, it is not at all uncommon for a woman to have mixed feelings** (for any number

25

of reasons) about the decision to end her pregnancy. The more difficult the decision, the more likely it is that the positive feelings about having the baby will resurface later, when the reasons for the abortion seem less compelling.

After three weeks of wavering between a desire to carry and a resolve to abort, Margaret finally agreed with her fiancé that a baby would completely disrupt their career plans. Once the procedure was over, she firmly put the episode behind her and plunged into finishing her MBA degree. The engagement didn't work out, but Margaret was successful in climbing the corporate ladder.

Twelve years later, Margaret found herself thinking about once-cherished dreams of marriage and children. Within one year she was married and vigorously threw herself into the happy task of getting pregnant—but she could not. As the months passed, Margaret found herself beginning to think more and more often of the baby so easily conceived years ago. The thoughts turned to yearning, and the yearning to a full-blown depression. And Margaret began, for the first time, wondering whether there was a corporate ladder high enough to climb away from the pain of going through the rest of her life childless.

2) **A woman having an abortion may be directly violating her own moral code.** Whether she has a mild uneasiness about abortion, or is violently opposed to it, any woman may reach a point where she feels that her own circumstances leave her no other option. (Nearly every abortion clinic director has some "war stories" about women who were picketing the facility one week and a client the next.[1])

Immediately after the procedure, such a woman will usually feel profound relief that the crisis is over, for better or worse. But any moral struggle she felt prior to the abortion will resurface eventually, at which point she will question her decision. The more intense the struggle, the more unpleasant the subsequent feelings are likely to be. In some cases, a woman who was originally comfortable with her abortion decision may undergo a change in moral perspective. This can also lead to uncertainty, if not outright grieving, about her past choice.

3) **A woman who feels that she was forced into the decision by others** (parents, boyfriend, husband) is likely to feel anger and bitterness later if and when her abortion becomes an issue in her life.

As a child Jean endured her parents' extremely stormy divorce, but as a result became a passive and dependent adult. Though attractive, she had difficulty with dating relationships and generally avoided them. She was, however, attracted to Alan, who was her opposite: self-assured, a smooth talker, used to having his own way. Even though he was several years younger than Jean, they met each other's needs and were soon married.

Alan had some very specific plans for their life together. Children were to be spaced far enough apart such that their home and his income would be sizable enough to accommodate them. As it turned out, Jean had trouble becoming pregnant, such that their first two children seemed to be minor miracles. When her daughters were 6 and 3, she began yearning for a third child, and even offered a tentative prayer to God that she might beat the odds once more. She did.

Alan was upset over the news of a future family member. The timing was wrong. He wanted each child to have an individual bedroom, and moving to a larger house was not on the agenda for this particular year. While his business income was more than adequate to handle expenses, a new baby simply did not fit into his plans. So, after very little discussion, he contacted a privately owned clinic in their community and scheduled Jean's abortion.

27

Jean did not do well at the clinic. On the morning of her appointment she wept openly as the consent forms were placed in front of her. The clinic staff, noting her obvious turmoil, sent her home to think it over. When Alan came home from work to find Jean still pregnant, he was furious. He made another appointment and personally took her back to the clinic, fuming about the time he had lost from his business to deal with this problem.

Jean's tears were no less obvious as the consent forms came out again, but now Alan stood by to make sure they were signed. He and the doctor both reassured her that "this was the right decision," and the abortion was completed. Months later, Alan could not understand why Jean was so distant, why she cried so much, and why she avoided making love.

Stories such as this seem to be far more common in abortion clinics than in private physicians' offices. Virtually all such facilities are ready and willing to support a woman through an abortion when others are pressuring her to have the baby. Some, however, are amazingly blind to the opposite situation, and will proceed with an abortion when an unhappy woman appears to be submitting to the pressure of others.

4) **Limited disclosure of details about the abortion procedure** (a practice particularly common in busy abortion clinics, where there may be little time or interest in prolonged explanations) may make the initial decision easier. But this may be a time bomb for some very unpleasant emotions later.

A woman signing a consent for abortion usually has only a vague idea about what will happen to her and the fetus. Without fail, there is no discussion about the size or state of development of the fetus, but rather the deliberate use of impersonal terms such as "pregnancy tissue" or "products of conception." Since the woman is usually in great turmoil about her decision, she is not likely to ask for too many details. She just wants to get the abortion over with.

Louise was 15 weeks into her pregnancy by the time she presented to an abortion clinic. Because of the late date, the clinic counselor said she would have a procedure called a D & E, which would be "just like the vacuum procedure." The abortion was scheduled for the end of the week.

Meanwhile a friend asked Louise to talk with the director of a local Crisis Pregnancy Center which offers information and services for alternatives to abortion. As it turned out, Louise had not actually been told what a D & E is. The initials stand for dilatation and evacuation of the uterus. At this stage of development, the fetus is too large to pass through the vacuum tube normally used in earlier pregnancies. The doctor must therefore use surgical instruments to remove the fetus a piece at a time. (Arms, legs, head, etc. must come separately.)

Louise was astonished to hear this basic explanation, insisting that none of this had been told to her at the clinic. Nevertheless, she still felt that she must have the abortion. The Crisis Pregnancy Center director challenged asked her to do one thing before the day of the appointment: return to the clinic and insist on a full description of the planned procedure, as well as specific information about the size and development of the fetus at 15 weeks.

One of the most common complaints of women who come to regret their abortions is that they didn't have all the facts, especially about the fetus growing inside them. At the time a woman may be comforted with a doctor's or counselor's talk about "products of conception," which gives the impression that an abortion does nothing more than remove a shapeless blob of cells. Later she may happen to watch a TV program about the first weeks of life (such as the excellent NOVA documentary "The Miracle of Life," which airs regularly on public television). Perhaps she will see similar images in a magazine or book. Whatever the source of information, the dawning awareness that what she aborted had arms, legs, a beating heart, and so forth can lead to agonizing questions: "Why didn't they tell me it looked like that? If I knew what I know now, I would never have had an abortion..."[2]

In 1983 two researchers reported some interesting observations in the prestigious *New England Journal of Medicine.* Two women were scheduled for ultrasound examinations of their early (10 week) pregnancies. The ultrasound allows a doctor to see the size of the fetus, as well as its motion, heartbeat, and other details. One woman had been punched in the abdomen, and had then had an x-ray done, just after becoming pregnant; the other had a possible problem with her hormone balance. Each was asked if she would like to watch the ultrasound screen, and if she would talk about what she saw. Both women had similar reactions to the procedure. The authors described one woman's response:

> She agreed without hesitation, indeed, with a spark of interest in her eyes. One of us pointed to the small, visibly moving fetal form on the screen and asked, "How do you feel about seeing what is inside you?" She answered crisply, "It certainly makes you think twice about abortion!" When asked to say more, she told of the surprise she felt on viewing the fetal form, especially on seeing it move: "I feel that it is human. It belongs to me. I couldn't have an abortion now."[3]

5) **Late abortions are more likely to be disturbing sooner or later** because the procedures are more complicated and the outcome looks much more like "killing a baby" than "extracting the contents of the uterus." This is especially true if the pregnancy has

progressed far enough to be visible, and if the woman has felt movement inside of her before the procedure.

After the fourth month, a pregnancy is ended by injecting a concentrated salt solution into the uterus. The fetus dies (often with vigorous kicking at first), and later the woman goes into labor, delivering what she can easily identify as a small, lifeless baby. The shock of this sight ("I didn't know it was a *baby!*") may cause her not only regret but a feeling that she was betrayed by her doctor or the abortion clinic. These experiences not only swell the ranks of groups such as Women Exploited by Abortion, but also lead to prolonged anger and bitterness.

6) **Issues related to wanted children later in life** can rekindle unpleasant aspects of the abortion decision. Most poignant is the situation of a woman who had one or more abortions earlier in life, and now is unable to become pregnant when she wants to. The thought of having aborted the only children she ever conceived will be a source of deepest pain and regret.

Similarly, a pregnancy with a wanted child may stir all sorts of memories and mixed emotions about a previous abortion. Focusing attention on the identity and health of the baby to be born raises some pointed issues. This pregnancy involves "my baby" which is to be nurtured and protected; the other consisted of "products of conception" which were destroyed. Realizing that they are biologically identical may be disturbing indeed.

7) **A woman who lives in an environment (such as a staunchly religious family) in which her abortion must be kept a deep, dark secret** is at greater risk for conflict at some point. While some might argue that her pain in such a case is the product of "repressive" surroundings, it is just as likely that she shares some of the anti-abortion sentiments of those around her.

• • •

One or more of the above situations can make the abortion decision and experience very emotionally charged. Once it is completed, the initial feeling immediately after the abortion is nearly always relief. For better or worse, a decision was made and the episode appears to be over. (It is this stage of a woman's experience that a number of studies have identified, without following the story further.)

But sooner or later, the issues which upset her previously will be raised again. Since she cannot go back and "undo" the abortion, one of two processes will begin. She may re experience emotional pain intense enough to drive her to seek help relatively soon after the procedure. Hopefully, she will find someone who can help her work through the process of healing, and will thus be spared a prolonged period of disturbance in her life.

On the other hand, she may encounter a counselor who will not acknowledge the significance of the abortion episode, thus leaving it unresolved. Or, more commonly, she may simply choose not to deal with it directly. In either case it is likely that she will employ one or more of the following defense mechanisms to protect her from uncomfortable thoughts and feelings:

1. **RATIONALIZATION** involves finding compelling reasons or excuses for having made the decision to abort. (Example: "It wouldn't have been fair to bring my baby into the world because I wasn't ready to be a mother—I probably wouldn't have been able to be a good mother at this point in my life".)

2. **REPRESSION** prevents unconscious information from reaching the conscious mind—blocking out memories of the painful emotions surrounding the abortion. (Example: "I did just fine with my abortion.

Sure, I may have been upset a little at the time, but it doesn't bother me at all now".) Sometimes a woman can push down not only the painful emotions but the actual details of the experience as well. Some have even "forgotten" that they had a second or third abortion.

3. **COMPENSATION** is an effort to make up for the abortion by "doing good things." (Example: being overly involved in church activities, working in the pro-life movement, becoming a "super mom," having an "atonement baby" soon after the abortion, etc.). It can also mean working very hard to prove that the abortion was really necessary. (Example: if a woman sacrificed her baby for a promising career, she might be heavily invested in making that career a great success.)

4. **REACTION FORMATION** involves pushing down frightening feelings and thoughts connected with a past abortion by strongly professing the exact opposite of those feelings—as if by expressing the contrary thought enough times, she can begin to believe it. (Example: becoming militantly vocal in the pro-choice movement).

These defense mechanisms are very effective in keeping the painful memories away, but they consume a lot of mental energy as a woman works to suppress powerful emotions. Eventually, if enough stress enters her life, she may find that she lacks the stamina both to cope with current stresses AND continue repressing "forgotten" memories. A variety of experiences (such as pictures of prenatal development, a subsequent pregnancy, or even the whine of a dentist's drill which resembles the sound of the abortionist's equipment) may then trigger symptoms associated with Post Abortion Syndrome.

1. The problem of the staunch pro-life woman who requests an abortion for herself or her daughter was discussed in a fascinating article in a widely circulated weekly newsmagazine for physicians. The report encompassed a broad range of women who make an abortion decision in opposition to their own moral standards. "Abortion Clinics' Toughest Cases," *Medical World News*, March 9, 1987, pp. 55-61.
2. Some (particularly pro-choice activists) have argued that disclosing details about the fetus does little more than make the abortion decision more difficult, and increases the risk for emotional suffering later. On the surface this viewpoint sounds valid. But it also flies in the face of the entire concept of informed choice. An consistent (and valid) goal of the feminist movement has been that of promoting a woman's full participation in medical decisions which affect her. It is ironic that most feminist literature objects to full disclosure about fetal development prior to abortion, preferring instead the old patronizing approach to women from health care providers. ("There, there, dear, don't worry about the details. Doctor knows best...")
3. John C. Fletcher, Ph.D and Mark I Evans, M.D., "Maternal Bonding in Early Fetal Ultrasound Examinations," *New England Journal of Medicine*, (*February 17, 1983*): 392-393.

Chapter Five:
The Symptoms of
Post Abortion Syndrome

C ounselors who have worked with postabortion women have seen a wide variety of complaints and emotional problems in their clients. These symptoms will not necessarily appear at the same time, nor is any woman likely to experience all of them. Some may occur immediately after an abortion, and others much later. However, if three or more of the symptoms listed below describe what you have recently experienced *in relation to a past abortion,* it is likely that you are experiencing Post Abortion Syndrome.[1]

GUILT: Guilt is what an individual feels when she has violated her own moral code. For the woman who has come to believe, at some point after an abortion, that she consented to the killing of her preborn child, the burden of guilt is relentless. There is little consolation to offer the woman who has transgressed one of nature's strongest instincts: the protection a mother extends to her offspring.

This inner voice of self-condemnation plays an accusing message in the mind over and over: *"You are defective. How could you have done this thing? You are a desperately wicked person."* It is also normal for many postabortion women entering therapy to verbalize their belief that any unhappy events which have occurred since the abortion were inevitable because they "deserve it." Many of the remaining symptoms listed below result from listening to this mental message day in and day out.

ANXIETY: Anxiety is defined as an unpleasant emotional and physical state of apprehension. Postabortion women with anxiety may experience any of the following: tension (inability to relax, irritability, etc.), physical responses (dizziness, pounding heart, upset stomach, headaches, etc.), worry about the future, difficulty concentrating, and disturbed sleep.

The conflict between a woman's moral standards and her decision to abort generates much of this anxiety. Very often she will not relate her anxiety to a past abortion, and yet she will unconsciously begin to avoid anything having to do with babies. She may make excuses for not attending a baby shower, skip the baby aisle at the grocery store, and so forth. This unrecognized "baby phobia" may eventually lead to a full-blown agoraphobia, where the mere act of leaving home creates great distress.

Carol entered therapy a year after her abortion, profoundly shocked at the levels of pain and anxiety she was experiencing. Every day she was taking eight to ten Xanax (a tranquilizer related to Valium) prescribed by a psychiatrist who had discounted her description of the pain surrounding her abortion experience. She had developed agoraphobia and was now in imminent danger of losing her job because of the panic attacks which occurred almost every day prior to leaving for work. Only when she came to realize that her present behavior was somehow connected to her abortion could Carol force herself to drive on the freeway, at night, to attend a postabortion therapy group.

PSYCHOLOGICAL "NUMBING": A person who has experienced a highly painful loss will develop an instinct to avoid future situations which might lead to serious pain again. Many postabortion women maintain an unverbalized vow that they will never again allow themselves to be put in such a vulnerable position. As a result, without conscious thought, they may work hard to keep their emotions on a flat level, experiencing neither highs nor lows. Not only does this flatness of emotional experience affect their own outlook, but it greatly hampers their ability to form and maintain close interpersonal relationships. It is not uncommon during therapy to hear a postabortion woman talk about her life as if it were happening to another person whom she watches go through all the motions of living.

Beth described her life this way: "I remember when I was younger I would wake up in the morning excited just to be alive in such a wonderful world. When we first got married things that happened to me either made me really happy or really sad. But after the abortion two years ago, it seemed like something turned off inside me. Nothing touches me anymore, good or bad. I can't get excited about things that used to put me in orbit, and now when I read about sad things that happen in the newspaper, I just think, 'Oh well, life comes and goes. It doesn't really matter. They'll get over it and keep on living.' I wish I could go back to the way I used to be. What's the use of going through life cold and indifferent to things that happen to you and around you?"

DEPRESSION AND THOUGHTS OF SUICIDE: All of us are acquainted with depression. It is a mood filled with sadness, guilt, and feelings of hopelessness. A more severe and prolonged depression is characterized by a sense of utter futility, and a complete inability to experience pleasure from any source. It may lead to suicidal ideas, as a person blames and hates herself so much that she simply wishes she were dead.

Few postabortion women reach the point of an overt clinical depression. Most continue to function and perform the duties of life, while still experiencing many of the following:

1. SAD MOOD - ranging from feelings of melancholy to total hopelessness.

2. SUDDEN AND UNCONTROLLABLE CRYING EPISODES - the source of which may be a total mystery to the woman, if she hasn't yet connected her present sad mood to memories of the abortion. The unpredictability and intensity of these crying spellsmay give rise to a sense of panic over being so out of control. A more severely depressed person may feel like crying but lack the energy to do so.

3. DETERIORATION OF SELF-CONCEPT - because she feels wholly deficient in her ability to function as a "normal" woman. These feelings of unworthiness are profound because she sees herself as unredeemable—a lost cause. She does not believe she can help herself, nor can anyone else help her.

4. SLEEP, APPETITE, AND SEXUAL DISTUR-BANCES - usually in a pattern of insomnia, loss of appetite, and/or reduced sex drive. On the other hand, sleeping and eating behaviors can become excessive. (It is unusual, however, for a woman to experience an increased sex drive during a depression. In fact, many postabortion women report pain with intercourse.)

5. REDUCED MOTIVATION - for the normal activities of life. The things that occupied her life before the depression (working, hobbies, reading, family life, friendships, and so on) just no longer seem worth doing.

6. DISRUPTION IN INTERPERSONAL RELA-TIONSHIPS - because of the general lack of enthusiasm for all activities. This is especially evidenced in her relationship with her husband or boyfriend, particularly if he was involved in the abortion decision. Anger can be stored against him even if he was "supportive of whatever she decided." A woman is often likely to resent his neutral stand when, in retrospect, she believes he should have been more protective of their child during a time when she

herself wasn't thinking clearly. A host of psychosexual disorders crop up in the aftermath of a couple's abortion, and they are far more likely to break up rather than stay together more than one year after the abortion.

7. THOUGHTS OF SUICIDE - or preoccupation with death. Not surprisingly, some postabortion women are so depressed that they have come to the point of believing they would be better off dead. If such a woman is able to verbalize the desire to end her life, and especially if she actually has a plan to do so, she is experiencing the severest form of clinical depression and needs immediate professional attention.

Emily described herself, during the first session of a postabortion therapy group, as being normally a very disciplined person. She was surprised by her emotional instability over the past several weeks. She said that she was avoiding meals, tossing and turning at night for the first time in her life, and crying in the middle of the day for no reason at all. She had become increasingly irritable with her two children and was easily distracted. (She described one incident where she went into the kitchen to prepare her son's lunch, then found herself standing in the middle of the kitchen, staring off into space, unable to remember what she had started to do). Most of all, Emily was terribly frightened because she had never experienced anything like this before. Her husband was becoming angry with her prolonged agitation over the abortion, and began to insinuate that maybe she was mentally unbalanced. After many weeks of fighting, Emily had come to feel that it was all quite hopeless and had given up trying to salvage the relationship.

She admitted in that first therapy session that she was toying with the idea of taking her own life, but didn't think she could overcome her strong sense of responsibility toward her children. She began to cry profusely as she confessed that even this sense of loyalty to her own children was beginning to crumble. After all, she sobbed, she wasn't a fit mother. Perhaps they would be better off raised by someone else.

It is important to remember that the symptoms listed above may be seen in *anyone who is depressed*. Post Abortion Syndrome may be the primary cause of the depression, or it may be but one of several contributing problems. Some work with an experienced counselor (hopefully one who understands PAS) may be necessary to put all of the components of a depression into perspective.

ANNIVERSARY SYNDROME: There tends to be an increase of symptoms around the time of the anniversary of the abortion and/or the due date of the aborted child. This phenomenon is reported with some consistency by women who are experiencing PAS.

REEXPERIENCING THE ABORTION: A common event described by postabortion women is the sudden onset of distressing, recurring "flashbacks" of the abortion episode. Sometimes this occurs in situations which resemble some aspect of the abortion. A routine gynecological exam is an obvious example, but even the suction sound of a household vacuum cleaner has been reported as a trigger for troubling flashbacks.

Sometimes women report an increase of "happy" baby dreams which leave them sad upon awakening and finding empty arms. More often, however, women re experience the abortion in the form of recurring nightmares about babies in general or her aborted baby in particular. These dreams usually involve themes of lost, dismembered, or crying babies. One woman described a nightmare in which the bloodied upper torso of her aborted child was clinging to the outside of her bedroom window at night, calling out to her mournfully, "Mommy, help me!" Another woman talked about a nightmare in which she was frantically trying to gather up all the pieces of her aborted baby and put them back together like a jigsaw puzzle. As gruesome as these dreams sound, they are not unrepresentative of the experiences shared in a postabortion therapy group.

PREOCCUPATION WITH BECOMING PREGNANT AGAIN: A significant percentage of women become pregnant within one year of their abortion. The desire to become pregnant again—as soon as possible—is verbalized often in the counseling room. This may represent an unconscious hope that a new pregnancy, often called the "atonement baby," will serve as a replacement for the one that was aborted.

ANXIETY OVER FERTILITY AND CHILD-BEARING ISSUES: Some postabortion women maintain a fear that they will never become pregnant again or carry a pregnancy to term. Some expect to have handicapped children because they have disqualified themselves as good mothers. Those women whose worldview includes a belief in God and divine accountability will often verbalize these fears in terms of God punishing them.

DISRUPTION OF THE BONDING PROCESS WITH PRESENT AND/OR FUTURE CHILDREN: The postabortion woman may not allow herself to become properly bonded to another pregnancy because of a fear of loss, as explained above. Or, she may begin another pregnancy intending to be the "world's most perfect mother" in order to make up for aborting the last pregnancy.

Likewise, the woman who already had children at the time of her abortion may discover that she is beginning to view her existing children in a different light. At one extreme, she may unconsciously "devalue" them. One woman sadly commented, "I always thought my children were the most prized possessions we had; now I catch myself looking at them while they are playing and thinking bizarre things like, 'You were the lucky ones. You were allowed to live.'"

She may go in the opposite direction and become overly protective. Another woman confessed that, since her abortion experience, she had become obsessively involved with her children, wanting to prove to the world and to herself that she was not a bad mother.

SURVIVAL GUILT: Few women abort for trivial reasons. They find themselves in the midst of a heartbreaking situation whereby they stand to lose much if they choose to carry their pregnancies to term. In the end, the decision boils down to a sorrowful conclusion: "It's me or you, and I choose me." In an attempt to assuage the guilt of being the "survivor," a woman will sometimes enter a heightened and unrealistic "compensation mode" whereby she attempts to atone for her choice.

She may keep herself very busy doing unselfish volunteer work. Indeed, she may become overly zealous in the pro-life movement. And this, unfortunately, may be the worst possible place for her to be. If she has not found forgiveness for her own abortion, she will not likely be able to extend compassion and forgiveness to anyone else who has aborted. All too often, "talking someone out of having an abortion" becomes her way of making payments on the debt she feels she owes. Any seasoned director of a Crisis Pregnancy Center has learned to screen out and refer for counseling the well-intentioned volunteer who hasn't worked through a past abortion. While postabortion women who have experienced healing and forgiveness are usually highly effective counselors, those who lack this experience of healing can turn a conversation with an abortion-minded woman into a disaster.

DEVELOPMENT OF EATING DISORDERS: Some women seeking postabortion counseling have developed eating disorders. While this phenomenon remains largely unexplored at this time, several factors may contribute to the correlation between abortion guilt and eating disorders. First, a substantial weight gain or severe weight loss is associated with unattractiveness, which reduces the odds of becoming pregnant again. Second, becoming unattractive serves as a form of self-punishment and helps perpetuate the belief that she is unworthy of anyone's attention. Third, extremes in eating behavior (such as bulimia or anorexia) represent a form of control for the woman who feels her life is otherwise out of control. And finally, a drastic weight loss can shut down the menstrual cycle, thus preventing any future pregnancies.

ALCOHOL AND DRUG ABUSE: Alcohol and drug use often serve initially as a form of self-medication—a way of coping with the pain of the abortion memories. One study found that 78% of women alcoholics reported some type of problem related to childbearing, contrasted with 34% of the married controls, and it is suggested that gynecological problems may contribute to doubts a woman has about her own adequacy as a female.[2] Sadly, the woman who resorts to alcohol and/or drugs eventually finds herself having not only more problems but also fewer resources with which to solve them. The mental and physical consequences of alcohol and drug abuse only amplify most of the symptoms the woman is already experiencing.

OTHER SELF-PUNISHING OR SELF-DEGRADING BEHAVIORS: The postabortion woman may also enter into abusive relationships, become promiscuous, fail to take care of herself medically, or deliberately hurt herself emotionally and/or physically.

Miriam's mother had originally told her she would support her daughter in whatever decision she made concerning her unplanned pregnancy. But two months after the procedure was done, Miriam's mother broke down one night, weeping over the abortion, hurling the accusation that "only a slut would sleep around and then callously abort." Already having emotional difficulties with the abortion decision, Miriam slumped into a deep depression. Waitressing at a local restaurant in the evening, she would begin drinking a while before her shift ended, and then go home with whomever looked like the most likely candidate for at least one night of pseudo-closeness. She knew this behavioral pattern was self-destructive, but she was willing to do anything to numb the pain of her mother's (and her own) accusations.

BRIEF REACTIVE PSYCHOSIS: Rarely, a postabortion woman will experience a brief psychotic episode for two weeks or less after her abortion. The break with reality and recovery are both extremely rapid, and in most cases the person returns completely to normal when it is over. While this is an unusual reaction to abortion, it bears mentioning only because it is possible for a person to have a brief psychotic reaction to a stressful event without being labeled a psychotic individual. During such an episode, the individual's perception of reality is drastically distorted.

One single woman, a respected professional who lived by herself in a small town, passed a very large piece of bloody material only hours after returning home from her abortion. She examined it and decided that it had to be her eight-week fetus. (She later reported that the clinic had been extremely busy the Friday she had gone in. Presumably, the physician neglected to make sure the fetus had passed through the suction tube, or perhaps she had been carrying twins.) Because she had, until then, believed that an eight-week fetus is an unidentifiable mass of tissue, the unmis-

44

takable human characteristics of the fetus sent waves of horror through her.

Using a soft kitchen towel, she carefully wrapped it up, decided it was a girl, gave her a name, and proceeded to rock her and talk to her during the next two days as if she were a live baby. By late Sunday afternoon, she began to acknowledge that her baby had died. She then drove out to the seaside, because she wanted to "bury" her baby in the ocean. A few hours later, she felt as though she were waking from a long dream. The fetus she passed had been real, but then she had experienced a total break from reality for nearly two days. Needless to say, she was badly shaken by the experience. Having heard that a local Crisis Pregnancy Center offered postabortion counseling, she came for help soon thereafter. She has not experienced any recurrences of psychotic episodes, brief or prolonged since that time.

---

1. It is important to remember that an abortion may not be the *ONLY* cause, but a contributor, to these symptoms.
2. Association for Interdisciplinary Research in Values and Social Change *Newsletter*, Vol. 1, No. 2, Winter, 1988, page 2.

Chapter 6:
The Task of Healing

*T*he experiences of many therapists who are now working with postabortion women show that time alone does not bring real, lasting healing. In fact, frequently the women who are most in need of help are those whose abortions took place years in the past. While a postabortion woman may have acquired enough coping skills to be a well-functioning member of society, she remains at risk for deterioration if the repressed pain surfaces in some way. When a woman comes to a point in her life where she recognizes the need to deal with a past abortion, a professional or lay counselor can be of great help in guiding her through the process of healing, either individually or in a group setting.

Therapists and researchers who have spent countless hours helping women deal with postabortion pain have consistently found that there are some basic task areas to be worked through for a person experiencing PAS to find relief. The specific *way* in which the work is done may vary considerably, but each task area must eventually be addressed. The ideal approach to dealing with any painful past episode is to involve a third person in the healing process—be it a friend, lay counselor or professional. The reason for this is obvious: if the event was emotionally painful, the mind has usually worked efficiently to tuck away the hurtful memories into some dark recess of the subconscious so that they will not be disruptive. It's difficult to deal with that negative information on one's own, because the mind automatically seeks to protect mental stability. A third party, however, is not as threatened by this information and can gently help a woman bring it into conscious focus where it can be dealt with decisively.

If you feel emotionally wounded from a past abortion experience, we hope that this chapter, in particular, will facilitate your healing process, whether or not you can find someone (or a postabortion support group) to help you. We realize that you may be in an area where there simply aren't many counselors available. It is our prayer that this information will encourage you at least to seek out a trusted friend, preferably someone with some spiritual insight, and share your pain with her.[1]

You may discover that you have already partially worked through one or more of the task areas. It is not uncommon, for instance, for the woman with a Christian worldview to understand (at least on an intellectual level) God's forgiveness, while refusing to admit that she has harbored anger toward those who played a coercive role in her abortion decision.[2] Another woman with no particular religious orientation may fully recognize her anger issues but be totally unaware that she has a spiritual hunger which needs to be addressed. Like every woman who goes through the postabortion healing process, you will progress through the tasks at different rates, needing to spend a great deal of time with one, and then perhaps finding another relatively easy to work through.

1. Working through the denial
(Reexperiencing the abortion):

The very first task of healing is to access the negative feelings that surrounded the abortion experience. Most women, even those currently experiencing a great deal of postabortion stress, have utilized repression for so long as a coping strategy that they have long "forgotten" the fear, anger, guilt and grief associated with the abortion. Until these powerful emotions are fresh in your mind again, there simply is not enough information to work with in order to accomplish the other tasks.

If you are hurting from a recent abortion you are probably thinking, "Are you kidding? There's nothing to 'access'—it's all here—fresh and painful. What I need is an anesthetic; if I *could* submerge it I *would!*" Obviously you haven't had time to employ one or more of the defense mechanisms which others have used for months and years following their abortions. Chances are, however, that the pain you are feeling right now is an *enraged* sort of pain. Your specific goal in this first task area will be to sort out and label the various feelings you are experiencing. You are probably well aware of your anger; but there are other hurts there as well. Responding to the kinds of questions listed in this section will help you begin.

If your abortion was in the more distant past, the most efficient way to access those feelings is to find a safe, supportive environment in which you can tell your story—whether to a counselor who knows about Post Abortion Syndrome, to a postabortion support group, or to an understanding friend who is willing to commit a good deal of time to help you.

Since you will naturally tend to avoid something you know will make you feel badly, a sensitive counselor or friend can help you reexperience the abortion, with some gentle prompting to help you persevere in remembering. It may be necessary for you to tell the story more than once, because the more often you are able to verbalize the abortion experience, the more details you will remember.

Here is a beginning list of questions to help you start this process. If you are by yourself, make sure you are in a comfortable, private place where you will be uninterrupted for as long as it takes. Write out your answers, and include some questions that you come up with yourself. If you have located a close friend or counselor who is willing to go through this with you, go ahead and write out your answers, and then go over them verbally with that other person.

1. How did you meet the father of the baby?

2. At the time you decided to have sex with him, what was your understanding about the relationship? What do you think his understanding was?

3. Did you ever talk together about the possibility of your sexual activity leading to pregnancy? Was there a mutual understanding as to what course of action would be taken if you got pregnant?

4. What did you feel when you first found out you were pregnant?

5. What was your boyfriend/husband's reaction? Friends' reactions? Parents' reactions? What did they want you to do?

6. What were your feelings about abortion before your pregnancy? Was you decision to abort a violation of your internal code of "right and wrong"?

7. How did you get to the abortion clinic? How did you feel as you were going there? What was said? What do you wish had been said?

8. What was it like in the waiting room? Describe the atmosphere around you and what the other patients seemed to be feeling.

9. What did the table feel like? What was going through your mind? Did you have second thoughts?

10. How would you describe the clinic workers? Were they understanding and sympathetic? What did you need from them that you didn't get?

11. How did you feel—physically and emotionally —while the abortion was being performed? What did you see? Smell? Hear?

12. How did you feel—physically and emotionally —when it was over?

13. What happened to the relationship with your boyfriend/husband after the abortion? With your parents? With any friend(s) who had an important role in your abortion decision?

14. What do you think is the most detrimental way abortion has affected your life?

15. If you were in similar circumstances today, would you make the same choice?

It is not unusual to answer these questions in a superficial way the first time you go through them. Your brain is extremely efficient in its ability to avoid confronting information that it knows will hurt, and so it may take a few attempts to access the old feelings. Put your answers away for a few days and then try again. The material you are looking for will have been moved closer to the surface by your earlier efforts. It is extremely common for women going through postabortion support groups to come back for the second or third session shaken by what they have suddenly remembered since the first telling of their story. (If you are attempting to counsel with a woman experiencing PAS, be very patient with the person who has difficulty accomplishing this first task.)

Tracy is an attractive professional in her mid 20s who came to a postabortion support group after attending counselor training at a local Crisis Pregnancy Center two months previously. She realized that the videos and information on fetal development had caused her a great deal of stress as she remembered her past abortions. She was very surprised at her reaction, because she assumed this was an issue she had dealt with long ago.

The first session closed as each member took 10 minutes to tell the group a little bit about her abortion experience. The women demonstrated varying degrees of sadness or anger, and some shed a few tears. Tracy was the last to share, and the description of her abortions was concise and completely devoid of any emotion, either in voice or body language. The rest of the group sat in deep compassion as she told of aborting 6-month-old triplets when she was 14 years old. She had been alone in a hospital room, with an angry, disappointed mom waiting downstairs, as she delivered her saline-aborted babies. One year later Tracy was pregnant, and aborted again.

She had never made the connection between these traumatic experiences and the overly-controlled manner in which she now conducted her life. After several subsequent attempts to access the emotions of those abortions, Tracy was frustrated. She felt she was highly motivated to cooperate with whatever the process required, but she couldn't seem to release the control which now held her back. Eventually, as the counselor had her inject words which conveyed feelings into every phrase of her story, 12 years of carefully curbed emotions began pouring out, and Tracy could now progress through the rest of the tasks. She is now leading a postabortion support group in her own town.

While Tracy's story may seem more dramatic than average, the numbness that had dominated her emotional life is, unfortunately, all too common in the women we see. Anyone who has ever gone through some deeply scarring event understands the indifference that is used to cover hysteria, as well as the tremendous fear of getting in touch with whatever is "down there." Tread gently, and with great compassion, with such a person.

2. Dealing with issues of guilt,
and accepting God's forgiveness

Jenny came to the Crisis Pregnancy Center in response to a yellow pages ad which offered "postabortion counseling." In filling out an initial questionnaire about her abortion experience, Jenny listed no particular religious affiliation, either currently or in her family background. Later in the questionnaire, however, she indicated that one of her strongest emotional reactions to the abortion experience was guilt, and feeling "terribly afraid that I've done something against God."

Maybe you're like Jenny and feel confused that you are suddenly thinking about God for the first time in years. Actually, it is very natural for you to be thinking about spiritual things right now, even if you wouldn't ordinarily describe yourself as a "religious" person. It has been our experience in counseling with postabortion women that very few people really hold a purely atheistic worldview.

Most women have some sort of concept of God and an afterlife, even though the definitions may differ widely. We think it is important to use this painful place in your life to discover and perhaps redefine your concept of God. One of our primary convictions in postabortion counseling is that long-term healing will come only when a woman has been reconciled with God. Those who are able to accept the concept of a personal God, and then ask for and receive his total and unconditional forgiveness, are the women most successful in wiping out their burden of guilt.

The woman with a Christian orientation often has a surprisingly difficult time accepting God's forgiveness for her abortion, whether it occurred before or after her commitment to Christ. If feelings of closeness to God were previously enjoyed prior to the abortion, no such feelings now exist, and she probably believes the relationship to be irreparable in view of her atrocious sin. How dare she presume to sit at His feet like an innocent child after what she has done? Working her way back into the periphery of His kingdom, in the lowest rank of privilege, may be the highest spiritual goal she can imagine.

Many women cannot tolerate these feelings for long, and turn away from the church completely. Others enter into an intense compensation mode, assuming that if they are "good" long enough, if they "prove themselves," God will surely forgive them someday. Of course, this is not a conscious thought process on her part. During therapy, however, a woman may startle herself by realizing that she has had a specific number of years in mind (usually five to seven) for a period of penance.

Norma was married at age 25. When she returned from a one-week honeymoon, she discovered that she was already seven weeks pregnant. In less than 24 hours, she, her husband and her doctor had calmly decided on and carried out an abortion, because they felt this would be a most inopportune time to have a baby.

Norma had been raised in a Christian home where there was a high regard for life, though she was not a committed Christian at the time of her abortion. This background provoked an internal struggle over the next ten years. For a while she convinced herself that she had been bullied into the decision. But, in fact, the decision had been made calmly and rationally, and eventually she took full responsibility for her choice. She had worked night and day in her church for the last five years since recommitting her life to Christ, and still could not begin to consider the idea that she might already be forgiven for the abortion.

One night, during a postabortion group therapy session, Norma was struggling with the idea of God's forgiveness. The leader asked her to think about what she expected from her young son whenever he did something wrong. "I want him to see the wrong action through my eyes—without denying that he did it or making lame excuses for why he did it," she replied. "And I want to know that he is truly sorry for what he did."

She was perplexed when the counselor asked if she ever remained cold and punishing toward her son once he had reached the point of true repentance. "Why on earth would I do that?" she asked. "He is my child—I love him!" Then she slowly began to realize that God, as her loving parent, had been patiently waiting five years for her simply to turn around and ACCEPT His forgiveness. She then wept tears of joyous healing.

The most essential task for the Christian postabortion woman, then, is to accept, on an emotional level, what she probably already knows on an intellectual level: that God's forgiveness is already complete and that she must reach out and grasp it firmly. There are, in fact, three aspects of forgiveness which are part of this "firm grasp": knowing who ultimately has paid the debt, allowing intimacy with God to be restored, and understanding the difference between punishment and consequences.

The question of debt repayment is illustrated by the story of the unfaithful servant in Matthew 18, who in some ways is like a postabortion woman seeking to work off her transgression. In this parable a servant asks his master for time to pay back a huge debt, rather than begging to have it forgiven. Unfortunately, the debt equals far more than the servant's entire lifelong earning potential! Similarly, you may have an unspoken notion that you are "doing time" for a past abortion. But how can you ever repay the loss? Like the man in the story, you owe a debt which you can never repay, no matter how long you work!

You cannot put the aborted child back together and give him or her life. You must stop trying to pay the debt, and accept the fact that it was paid by Christ's death on the cross 2,000 years ago. There is no point in struggling with guilt and repayment. Instead, accept the only gift that brings freedom from guilt.

Restoring intimacy is the second aspect of forgiveness. It is perhaps best understood in our own parent/child relationships. One January a dear artist friend of ours gave us a late Christmas present: a miniature nativity scene which she had carefully sculpted from fragile clay. It was a precious gift, and a unique reminder of the one who made it. I brought it home, set it out on the dining room table, and told the children about it as I tucked them into bed.

The next morning, however, didn't start out well. Our 11-year- old son, Chad, was in an uncharacteristically bad mood, looking for a shirt that I hadn't had time to wash. Words he didn't really mean spilled out of his mouth, and I reprimanded him. He flounced angrily down the stairs and I followed, just in time to see him jerk his loaded backpack from the dining room table. Unfortunately, his backpack swept away the beautiful nativity scene onto the floor, with broken arms, halos and heads flying everywhere. We both stared in silent horror at what had occurred.

What happened in the next few minutes was a fascinating microcosm of human behavior. Chad's first reaction, as he realized I had witnessed the accident, was to rationalize: "Look what happened! Why did you put that *there*? It wouldn't have happened if you had put it in a safer place. It's not my fault!" Still stunned by what I had just seen, I didn't yet have the words with which to respond to this absurd protest, so I remained silent. And within a matter of minutes,

Chad's useless rationalizations melted as genuine repentance overwhelmed him.

Now, what do I, as a loving parent, want from my child when he has done something wrong? I want for him to see the deed for what it was and to take responsibility for his behavior. Most of all, I need to see genuine sorrow for what he has done. If these thought processes are in place, the path to reconciliation is completely cleared. Could I have extended forgiveness to my son if he didn't believe it was his fault? Could I have ignored the situation and expected our relationship to continue on a close and honest level? Of course not. Chad would have carried that guilt around until he finally dealt with it, because it would have created a barrier in our relationship (a highly uncomfortable state of affairs for an 11-year-old).

And what if, at the point of Chad's genuine repentance, I had responded with cold harshness, saying cruel things to him to vent the anger I was feeling about my broken nativity scene?[3] What if I had withheld my love and forgiveness until he could earn enough money to replace the broken gift, or until I was satisfied by a long period of "good behavior"? Is this the response of a loving parent? Unfortunately, it is all too often the response of a great many parents. And it is from our own parents that we form our concept of God as a heavenly parent. For many people, this leads to a very warped idea of how God operates.[4]

One of the most touching illustrations of God's forgiveness is found in the familiar parable of the prodigal son (Luke 15). After squandering his inheritance, the son eventually finds himself starving in a pig pen. As he begins to remember the benevolence of his father's household, and the kindness his father showed even the lowliest of servants, he comes to repent of the terrible decisions he has made. Knowing, however, that he doesn't deserve to be received back as a son, he formulates a plan whereby he will return to his father and beg to be hired as a servant.

Meanwhile, the father has been at the gate every day since his son left, hoping and praying that he will return. And now, suddenly, a weary figure trudges toward the estate. In great joy the father receives him back, sparing no expense with the "welcome home" party, and lavishing him with expensive gifts. In response to the son's prepared speech requesting a place among the servants, the father replies, "Nonsense! You are my *son*, and I am so overjoyed to have you home!"

Have you ever felt like that son? Are you finally at the place where you are ready to stop making excuses and rationalizations as to why you had to have the abortion? Do you just want to "go back home," longing for the days before all this pain started? Maybe, like the son, you have written off the possibility of enjoying a close relationship with God, but would be happy to just be "in the camp." Teri has heard women actually verbalize that they would be content if they could just be allowed to participate on the periphery, like a foot soldier who is unknown to the general but still part of the army.

Have you felt that you didn't deserve a special, personal relationship with God, that you didn't deserve to call him "Abba" ("Dad")? That feeling of self-condemnation does not come from God, who stands "by the gate" every day waiting for you to come home.

Finally, as you are dealing with the pain of ongoing memories you may be confusing the consequences of your abortion with punishment. In the story of the prodigal son, there was no punishment given by the father. On the other hand, neither could he magically create a new endowment for his son. Although the relationship was completely restored, the son had to live for the rest of his life knowing that he had wasted his inheritance money. The father could soften that blow somewhat by providing for him, but the squandered fortune was gone.

If you are a parent, you can probably think of a time when your child made an irresponsible decision that brought consequences you would have liked to reverse, but were powerless to do so. I am reminded of the time our daughter Carrie took our extremely tame but dim-witted cockatiel out of his cage in the back yard. She believed that he would be content to stay on her shoulder as he always had while in the confines of the house. But when this bird felt the sunshine on his shoulders, he was history! He soared on unclipped wings to the freedom of the skies, and was never seen again.

Was Carrie absolutely and genuinely sorry for taking the bird out of the cage? Absolutely. She fully understood the foolishness of her action. She was brokenhearted and her remorse continued for months after the incident. And as brokenhearted as I was for Carrie, there was utterly nothing I could do to bring that blasted bird back (although, for her sake, I would have paid good money to see him return). Carrie begged forgiveness for letting him out, and the family forgave her instantly, but she had to live with the painful consequences of that action for a very long time.

God, as a loving parent, is as grieved over your abortion choice as you now are. He feels your pain and has no desire to make you suffer more than you already have. What you have experienced is not a punishment from him, and hopefully it will not separate you from him.

There are many women who, though coming to understand the loving, forgiving nature of God, are seemingly unable to move through this important second task. To trust fully is a frightening proposition for someone who has never experienced the joy of a trusting relationship with a father (or any other man, for that matter). Additionally, some women unconsciously choose not to accept God's forgiveness. Holding on to one's "defectiveness" can become a rationalization for failing to move forward as a new, whole, healthy, person who is responsible for her present behavior. It may be time for you to leave behind your shroud of reasons why you are such a "bad," defective person, and instead decide to believe what God has said about his ability to forgive whatever you've done and make you whole.

If you just can't seem to work through this second task, work on the anger issues involved with your abortion decision and come back to this task.

3. Anger and forgiveness toward herself and others

Most women experiencing Post Abortion Syndrome have a tremendous amount of anger that has been suppressed since the time of the abortion. There is usually serious resistance to getting in touch with this dark emotion and identifying it for what it is. Sometimes this is caused by a fear that expressing anger will lead to rage and then a total loss of control. The Christian woman is often especially hampered in this task area, because she has heard countless sermons in which she has been exhorted not to harbor resentment toward another human being, but rather to forgive others as she has been forgiven by Christ.

The biblical command to forgive others as we have been forgiven is indeed a deep and beautiful truth. Unfortunately, until we can identify precisely what needs to be forgiven, it lays beneath the surface like a pool of toxic waste material, ever threatening to bubble up and poison our desperate striving for wholeness. The postabortion woman must stop denying the pain and anger she felt (and feels) before, during, and after her abortion. Recognizing anger clears the path to genuine and permanent forgiveness.

Elisa's mother and father had coerced her into getting an abortion when she was fifteen years old. In the postabortion therapy group, she denied, sweetly, any traces of bitterness against her parents, even though they had refused to discuss the episode with her over the years. As an adult, she knew that what they had done was wrong, but she believed that, as a Christian, she had no grounds for harboring any resentment toward them.

She shocked herself when she was asked to write a pretend letter to her parents telling them how she felt about their part in the abortion decision. The rage she expressed in writing distressed her greatly, because she honestly didn't know where it had come from. As she began talking about the contents of the letter in group one night, she slowly realized that the anger she had unconsciously held against her parents all these years had created a tremendous rift in her relationship with them.

That night she made a conscious decision to stop blaming them for the abortion, and the path to true forgiveness was now wide open. She had a long talk with them before the group ended, and joyously described to us the tears of reconciliation that were shared between the three of them. They had wanted, for years, to explain to her that their motivation for urging her to get an abortion had been love and concern for her future. Realizing their horrible mistake, they had wanted to talk to her about their failure, but had been unable to bring themselves to the point of addressing the issue.

Part of the work in this task area involves not only admitting that the anger is there, but also deciding what kind of anger you are holding. There is an unjustified anger in which you may choose to blame everyone and everything for your abortion, absolving you from taking responsibility for the abortion decision. Are you willing to be unhappy and miserable for the rest of your life because of someone else's actions? (This "someone else" could be a person who is long gone, and doesn't even remember your name.)

There is a different, more useful kind of anger that says, "I can take responsibility for my choice, recognizing that those who should have been the most helpful during this time in my life actually assisted me in making a decision that ultimately hurt me." The difference is in the concept of *shared* blame. As long as you refuse to admit any responsibility for the abortion, you will always be the perennial victim, who cannot control anything that happens to you. When you finally come to the point of acknowledging your responsibility and accepting forgiveness, your happiness and wholeness no longer depend on anyone else's bad choices. And you are suddenly free to forgive others who were involved.

An important part of this task is identifying those who are the targets of your anger. The possibilities could include the father of the aborted baby, a parent, a close friend, the abortionist, yourself, God, etc. And sometimes your anger can be directed at someone who had nothing to do with your abortion at all— such as a current boyfriend or husband.[5]

A good beginning exercise in this task area might be to list all of the people who had anything to do with your abortion experience. Next, draw a circle on a piece of paper; this is the "pie of responsibility". Using a pencil with an eraser, assign what you consider a fair piece of pie to each person on your list (use the whole pie—no pieces left over). Use your eraser and keep reworking this drawing until you have, in your judgment, an honest appraisal of what size piece goes to each person. Who has the biggest piece? Who has the smallest?

Next, write each person on your list a pretend letter that begins, "Dear _____: I am angry with you because..." (don't forget yourself!). Often a woman will be angry at someone, not for promoting the abortion decision, but for taking the ever popular stand, "I'll support you in whatever you decide to do." Many women in the postabortion support groups have expressed deep and bitter resentment against a boyfriend or husband who thought he was doing the modern thing by letting the choice be hers, when instead she desperately wanted him to say, "This is our baby—the product of our love. We'll make this work somehow." She feels he should have been strong at a time when she was most vulnerable, and her hostility runs deep.

During the first session of the group, Jolene quietly described her abortion of 13 years ago, involving a young man to whom she had been engaged. She automatically assumed they would simply move the wedding date up, but he argued vehemently for an abortion. Numbed with shock, she gave in rather than gamble on his walking out on the relationship. Two weeks before the wedding, he walked anyway. Three years later Jolene married another man with whom she now enjoys a fair relationship. They have wanted to have children, but Jolene has miscarried twice.

In response to the group's outraged questions about her feelings toward the father of the child she aborted, Jolene stated that she had never felt any anger toward him. The group sat back in disbelief. Three sessions later, after working on the anger chapter in the Women in Ramah workbook, she confessed that there might be some residual anger, after all. And by the time she got to the assignment of writing a pretend letter to this man, her wrath had grown to volcanic proportions. She spent an hour one night during the group vomiting up the foul feelings she had harbored against him for the past 13 years.

The sheer magnitude of her anger was frightening to Jolene, who had spent so many years denying that it even existed. What she hadn't realized was that her anger toward the faithless fiancee had seriously impaired her ability to form a close, trusting relationship with her husband. By the time the group had ended, she had released forever the anger toward her old boyfriend, started marriage counseling with her husband, and has experienced tremendous growth in their relationship. They are still hoping to have a baby someday.

It is interesting that sometimes a postabortion woman can easily extend compassion toward other members of the therapy group but be unable to forgive herself. Pointing out the inconsistency between her behavior and her thinking, coupled with the understanding and compassion felt from the rest of the group, will often help a woman relinquish her entrenched self-recrimination.

Liza met her husband while he was still in the midst of divorce proceedings. She became pregnant but did not tell him for fear of putting too much pressure on him during a time in his life that was already too stressful. Because it was 1956, Liza performed an illegal abortion on herself by inserting a sharp instrument through her cervix. She almost bled to death before finally getting to a hospital, where a physician angrily completed the botched abortion, verbally abusing her during the procedure for attempting such a stupid thing. Being a staunch Catholic, Liza was deeply ashamed of what she had done, and never told anyone about it until she entered a postabortion therapy group 31 years later.

She put off telling her story to the group as long as possible. When she finally did start talking, she could not bring herself to reveal that she had actually tried to abort herself. After much gentle urging from the counselor, she finally blurted out her confession and put her hands over her face, waiting for the condemnation she knew would come. To her great surprise, the other women silently wept in sorrow for the turmoil she must have felt to be driven to such a desperate act, and for the burden she had carried alone for so many years. For Liza, the fact that these women were readily able to love her, no matter what she had done in the past, was a major turning point in her being able to forgive herself.

As a last word of caution, it is important to keep in mind what the purpose of this task area. The purpose is *not* to create anger and bitter resentment where none previously existed. The purpose is *not* to have a "primal scream" type of therapy session in which everyone shouts obscenities at people who are no longer around. The purpose is to understand that unacknowledged anger allows us to keep blaming others for our failures. As soon as we see the anger for what it is, and to whom it is directed, we begin to understand that it is either unjustified and needs to be released, or justified, in which case we need to forgive the other person.

In almost every postabortion group, this question comes up: "Should I go to _____ and tell him/her that I have forgiven them?" There is no black and white answer to that question. You must ask yourself, "What is my motivation for telling this person? What do I think can be gained? Am I likely to get what I am seeking from this person?" If you haven't had contact with the father of your baby for some time, chances are he doesn't really care about the forgiveness you're extending him. Such an exercise would be futile at best, and perhaps even destructive. On the other hand, if the father of your baby is someone with whom you have had ongoing contact, and the pain between you has never stopped, by all means this is probably the time to talk to him about this.

If you feel "stuck" in this task area and can't seem to release the anger you feel toward someone, perhaps you have come to the point where you must ask what you are "buying" with that anger. Is it scary to think about living as a whole, responsible person, without making excuses for your bad choices because of the way someone else victimized you? Or perhaps you feel that becoming a whole person would be disloyal to your aborted child. Perhaps feeling ugly and angry toward yourself and others is part of your "penance." If you have an emotional reaction to any of these statements, you need to consider the possibility that something inside of you needs to hold on to that damaged self-concept. Remember, if God has forgiven you, what basis do you now have for withholding forgiveness from yourself? And if you have forgiven yourself, what basis do you now have for withholding forgiveness from anyone else?

4. Grieving the loss of the aborted child

Anyone who has lost a loved one knows how woefully inadequate are the comments from those who have never suffered a loss: "Well, at least he's with the Lord now." "Aren't you glad she won't be in pain anymore?" Friends flock around the bereaved one with sympathetic attention...for about two to four weeks. After that, life is supposed to be resumed as always.

For those who experience pregnancy loss through miscarriage, prenatal death or stillbirth, the litany of thoughtless remarks is worse: "It's just as well, honey; miscarriage is the body's way of rejecting a defective fetus." "Good thing you're young—you've got lots of time to have as many children as you want." "Aren't you glad you didn't carry it any longer than you did?" And the time of mourning (especially for the woman who miscarries early in the pregnancy) is callously reduced to the time needed to recuperate physically. The person who has never lost a pregnancy cannot begin to understand that a woman who has lost one will carry around a little hole in her heart for the rest of her life.

For those who have lost a child through abortion, the public awareness of the need to grieve the loss of that child is utterly nonexistent. The woman herself usually cannot identify that need. Hindering her in this important task of healing are (1) the belief that, as the one who decided on the abortion, it would now be hypocritical for her to presume to mourn the baby's death, (2) the fact that she has no memories of a whole child to facilitate a healthy grieving process, and (3) societal denial of the need to grieve what was, after all, only a "lump of pregnancy tissue."

The ache for the child that was aborted is nowhere better described than in Ally Sheedy's poem "Local Anesthesia": "I wish I could shake him off me...I know how hard he clutched me from the inside when they took him out. Now he dances bodiless tapping round my head like rain. When it was over I lay so still they thought I was in shock. But I was only saying good-bye to him. And you never can. 'Cause, child, I hear you in my head and on you cry like rain and I can feel you at my heart; inside I nurse you still."[6]

It is crucial for a postabortion woman to come to a point of understanding that she aborted a real human baby. Unlike the mother who has lost a two-year-old, the postabortion woman has no memories of her child. And since a healthy grieving process requires those warm sensory memories, it is often necessary to help a woman "recreate" her baby—pretending she knows his or her physical characteristics .in order to plant a mental and emotional picture firmly in her mind.[7] Naming the child also seems to be an important task, because it gives her child individuality.

With a portrait now indelibly etched on her heart, she can begin the difficult task of asking her child's forgiveness for the abortion. This can be a very frightening experience for the Christian woman who pictures her child now standing next to God, stretching an accusing finger down toward earth. This picture, of course, adds to her feelings of alienation from God. A woman must come into a realization that nobody in God's presence could reflect anything but His love, compassion, and forgiveness.[8] After an emotional and tender reconciliation with the child she never knew, after she feels that her child has already forgiven her, she will finally be in a position to say good-bye to her baby...for now.

It cannot be overstated that the purpose of this process is *not* to have a woman attempt to communicate with her dead child in some way. She should understand this very clearly. Furthermore, the imagining of the child's characteristics does not presume that she is contacting an "inner guide" from her subconscious mind. Also, the imagination process is not intended to manipulate external reality in any way. Rather, this is a technique to help a woman express her feelings about a real child—a necessary part of the grieving process. In addition, this exercise helps a woman gain a clear understanding of where her children are, and what their relationship will be some day when they are reunited.

A wonderful technique to help her facilitate this step is to encourage her to write a pretend letter to her aborted child, pouring out her heart and explaining (but not excusing) the circumstances under which the abortion was obtained. She might tell the child how much he or she is missed, how sorry she is, how she longs to see him or her someday, and so forth. Here is an edited version of an actual letter:

"Dearest Baby: I don't know how to begin writing this letter to you. I hope it's okay to think of you as a girl, because I always believed in my heart you were. You know, I only had your two brothers after I was pregnant with you, and I always wanted a daughter. I would have named you Dawn, and when I picture you, I see you with brown curls tied up in pigtails with pretty ribbons, and big, big blue eyes, just like mine...Baby Dawn, what can I say to tell you how sorry I am that I don't have you to hug or to dress or to put ribbons in your hair? I was so young and frightened when I found out you were growing inside of me. I allowed some foolish people to talk me into killing the only daughter I ever had, and I have to live with that for the rest of my life...I'm so happy you're with Jesus now. For a long time now Heaven has seemed like a really scary place to me because I was afraid of seeing you again, but lately I've begun to understand that you understand and have forgiven me. I can't wait to hold you one day. Good-bye, my precious daughter..."

---

1. We strongly advise that male friends or lay counselors, even with the best intentions, avoid working with postabortion women. The subject matter is difficult, dealing, among other things, with details of sexual experiences which a woman may find awkward to disclose to a man. In addition, some postabortion women harbor anger toward men (boyfriends, husbands, abortionists, etc.) which may cloud the discussion.

2. Sometimes, as she observes Christians in the group experiencing God's forgiveness, there arises in a non-Christian woman a yearning for that same reconciliation with her Creator. A Christian counselor needs to be prepared to explain, in the simplest of terms, how to grasp hold of this forgiveness.

3. For the sake of historical accuracy, I must confess that, while I did forgive Chad that morning, it took me a full day to work through my feelings of grief and anger over the episode. How grateful I am that God's forgiveness is instantaneous and perfect!

4. Two excellent books which review the various ways people view God are *Your God Is Too Small*, by J. B. Phillips and *The Father Heart of God*, by Floyd McClung, Jr.

5. Women who come into a postabortion group often express frustration and anger when their husband/boyfriend does not support their attending the group. If the husband/boyfriend was the father of the aborted baby, he may have his own postabortion issues with which to deal, He may resent the fact that his wife/girlfriend is "stirring the pot" again by deliberately focusing on an episode he would prefer to be forgotten. If the husband/boyfriend was *not* the father of the aborted baby, he may feel resentful that his wife/girlfriend wants to spend time in a group where she is going to discuss her prior sexual relationship with another man.

6. Sheedy, Ally, *Yesterday I Saw the Sun*. New York, New York: Summit Books, 1991.

7. An issue that seems to come up with some regularity in the counseling room is the question of the current developmental stage of the child. Should she think of him or her as a preborn fetus, a newborn baby, the age he/she would now be, or an adult? While most women progressing through this task naturally prefer to think in terms of a small baby, it is important for her to understand that, no matter what the child looks like physically, he or she certainly has the same perceptual awareness of an adult at this point. See I Corinthians 15:35-44. Also Phil. 3:20-21.

8. We cannot recommend strongly enough the book *Tilly* by Frank Peretti to help a woman work through this task area (be careful to not introduce this tape until she has worked on the other task areas). Focus on the Family produced a dramatization of this story on audio cassette which is equally moving (write and ask for the "Tilly" tape).

Chapter 7:
How Do I Deal with the Ongoing Memories?

*H*aving successfully worked through these major task areas, will you ever feel pain over your past abortion again? Most likely. It is unrealistic to expect that someone who has grieved deeply will never again come up against painful reminders of her loss. The goal is for you to become a whole, functioning person who is able to cope with those ongoing reminders when they arise, rather than feeling overwhelmed by them.

Many times, while lecturing on this subject around the country, I have met women during a break who ask fearfully, "How do I know if I've been healed from my abortion experience? I thought I had dealt with it pretty well two years ago, and I'm really surprised at how emotional I've become while listening to you today. I came here because I thought I was ready to run a postabortion support group, but now I'm having real doubts. Have I just been kidding myself?"

A woman who has worked diligently through all the task areas of healing may be upset when some old and confusing feelings suddenly confront her. Most often she will question whether the work she completed earlier was legitimate. (Because this occurs so often during seminars on Post Abortion Syndrome, we now address this issue at the beginning of any talk.)

Sometimes a return of symptoms may indicate that you need to complete one or more of the task areas. For instance, I have worked with many women who seemed to have successfully dealt with issues of guilt and forgiveness, but who never recognized their deep need to grieve the loss of their aborted child. I have talked to other women who have been completely uninhibited about mourning their loss, but who have harbored a deep-rooted bitterness against those who pushed her toward the abortion. If you have only partially worked through the task areas, then it is natural and understandable that you will feel anxious and fearful as you approach what is uncharted territory.

It has often been observed that we live in an "instant" society. This cultural expectation for immediate results extends, unfortunately, into the universe of those who grieve. So it is natural that the woman who has finally faced the pain of a past abortion, worked through the tasks, and experienced substantial healing will be bewildered at the first sign of returning painful memories. "Once healed, always healed" is a fantasy. In reality, the painful memories may return again and again.

One of the most important gifts a counselor can give to the woman who has just spent weeks and perhaps months working through her abortion pain is the understanding of the healing process. A simple analogy may help clarify this process.

Imagine for a moment that your mind is a beautiful oak roll-top desk in a California home. Stuffed into dozens of small slots and pigeon-holes in that desk are all your ugly abortion memories—the ones that you hurriedly crammed into those various odd places so long ago because you needed desperately for your desktop to look clean, and you didn't want to go through the hard work of organizing the mess. At first it may not have been hard simply to throw them here and there. But as months and years passed, and you continued to stuff the slots with life's disappointments and pain, now it takes quite a bit of effort to cram anything else into the desk.

Suddenly a large earthquake erupts, and all of the contents of those dark pigeon-holes are mercilessly thrown all over the desk. What a mess! Can you stuff them back into the holes? Or is the mess now so extensive that this is no longer possible? Suppose you decide to go through the agonizing process of sorting through the entire, chaotic pile. One by one you pick up bits and scraps of long-forgotten feelings and deal with them, thoughtfully deciding where each item belongs. This difficult job finally done, your desktop is not only neat, but the "hidden" parts of your desk are completely organized and dealt with.

But, as every Californian knows, after a major earthquake comes a series of aftershocks. So half of what you labored so hard to organize comes tumbling back onto the desktop. But this time it doesn't take nearly as long to recover from the situation, because you have already done the major work. You now know where everything belongs and the process of restoring order will not take as long this time.

In just the same way, the person who has made the choice to work through the painful process of sorting out the guilt, fear, anger, and grief of a past abortion is going to experience "aftershocks." When they occur, you need not panic. You must, however, sit down immediately and deal with the feelings that are reemerging. The work has been done before, so it's not going to be as traumatic, nor should it cause as much disruption in your life as the initial "quake" (unless there remains a task area which has not been explored).

Even though aftershocks may be a problem, there are also some observable characteristics which indicate that someone has experienced substantial healing from PAS:

1. There is a rapid decrease in symptoms as she resumes normal functioning in her life. Not only does she "pick up where she left off" before the increasing symptoms brought paralysis into her routine, but she should be functioning at a higher level because her ability to maintain close, personal relationships will have improved. Having confronted the role of denial in her life, she is now more honest in dealing with her feelings, and thus has greater ability to communicate with those closest to her (spouse, boyfriend, children, parents, etc.). In short, she has a whole different countenance and it is noticeable even by those who don't know what she's gone through.

Gina, 32, had been married 10 years but had never told her husband about the abortion she had when she was 15. One of the greatest fears in her life was that her husband would no longer love her in the same way if he knew she had consented to an abortion. So she chose not to reveal her secret. But as the years passed and the stresses of life piled up, Gina began resenting a relationship built on the conditional love she imagined her husband to have for her. ("I love you only because you are so wonderful", she imagined him thinking.) The longer this continued, the more Gina decided that her husband was incapable of handling the truth.

Balanced dangerously between an irrational but growing disappointment with her husband and an unwillingness to test his love by telling him, many areas of her life became increasingly disrupted, until she finally sought help through a postabortion group. Over time, the group helped her through one of the hardest tasks of her life: confiding with her husband about her previous abortion. His understanding and compassionate response dispelled all of her preconceived beliefs about how he would react, and their marriage relationship today is built on an honesty they had never previously enjoyed. And because of that healed

74

relationship, Gina's capacity for dealing with the normal routines of life has been greatly enhanced.

2. She can speak openly about her abortion experience when it is appropriate to do so. There is nothing quite so touching as a woman who can talk about her past abortion and subsequent healing without being afraid of what people might think. This is the woman who has been set free by the knowledge that her slate has been wiped completely clean. The exhilaration of this heart knowledge is so powerful that it completely eclipses any former fear of someone learning her deep, dark secret.

To balance this statement, it must be pointed out that most women who have gone through the healing process will *not* choose to address large groups on this topic. (Indeed, the pro-life community must be very careful to guard against exploiting these women by pressuring them to speak at public functions). In fact, if a woman seems to demonstrate a compulsive need to address groups in order to give excruciating details of her abortion experience, she may be trying to "do penance" through this repeated verbal self-abuse. The woman who has experienced healing will find herself willing (though not necessarily eager) to share her story in any situation where she judges the hearer(s) will benefit from her narrative.

3. She uses owning, non-blaming language when talking about her abortion experience. Because she has stopped rationalizing her abortion, the woman who has known healing can simply admit she made a wrong choice—a wrong choice for which she has experienced total forgiveness. There is no trace of accusation (toward herself or others) in her tone of voice or description of what happened to her.

Arlene was 14 years old when a close friend of the family sexually abused her, convincing her it would be useless to tell anyone because "no one believes kids—they lie and exaggerate." Over the next four years, Arlene became heavily involved with drugs and overeating. When she became pregnant, her "boyfriend" blamed her for the pregnancy, informed her she would have to pay for the abortion, and disappeared. She was married and divorced within one year of her abortion.

Arlene's life became a downward spiral of drugs, drinking, promiscuity, and self-hatred. The merry-go-round ended with an overdose of tranquilizers, and a 18-hour coma in the Intensive Care Unit. Realizing finally that she had hit bottom, Arlene started attending church for the first time in many years. She heard about post-abortion counseling offered in a local center and attended group sessions.

Today she is involved in helping other postabortion women work through the healing process. One of the highlights of watching these women enjoy wholeness again is witnessing a soft-spoken, beautiful young woman like Arlene speak publicly about her experience in a very straightforward manner, without anger and without blame.

4. She accepts God's unconditional and total forgiveness. She is also able, finally, to forgive herself completely, and to extend forgiveness and/or understanding toward others who assisted and supported her abortion decision. She has completely relinquished any traces of doubt that she is forgiven, entirely and eternally. She has stopped playing the accusing mental "tapes" which told her for so long that she would never be absolved of such a hideous crime. Having grasped the beautiful reality of forgiveness, she finds it difficult to hold on to any grudges toward others.

She now understands that the burden of guilt for anyone else who was involved is an issue which will have to be resolved by that person alone. Nothing she can do will affect how another person will process the abortion (except, when appropriate, letting the other know of her own healing experience and of her forgiveness and release of that person).

5. If married, she relates differently to her spouse. Most postabortion women experience some degree of communication problems and sexual dysfunction in their marriage relationship, whether or not her husband was the father of the aborted baby. If she feels unforgiven and unredeemable, this deeply affects her ability to enter into a close marital relationship as a whole person. It is likely that she is either too needy or too self-protective and distant. In either case, the effect on the marriage is devastating over the course of many years.

Once a woman has dealt with the self-hatred, the anger, and the grieving involved with the abortion, she is well on her way to becoming a whole person who can allow herself to be vulnerable and intimate.

6. She can now deal with other issues in her life. I have never worked with a woman for whom a past abortion was the only source of pain in her life. The downward spiraling self-concept can lead to other self-defeating life choices. Perhaps she is trying to cope with other issues that have just simply been too painful to look at until now. Maybe there was a history of sexual abuse in her past that has been a secret for so long she hasn't known how to approach a healing.

The healing journey for a past abortion is no different than for other issues. Anger, grief, shame, feeling unforgiven by God—these are the issues which have to be confronted no matter what the issue. But once she has experienced forgiveness and release of anger for her past abortion, it won't be as difficult to now approach other problems.

7. She feels reconciled with her aborted child. For the Christian woman this is an especially important indication of her inner healing, because she knows she will meet this child again someday. If she expects this reunion to be painful, or if she cannot be assured that her child is whole and happy and at perfect peace, then the prospect of life and relationships after death will be terrifying. But the woman who has accepted *all* of God's forgiveness through Christ can look forward with wistful anticipation to being reunited with her child, and is now free to enjoy a close relationship with God during the rest of her earthly life.

8. She is able to deal successfully with the ongoing memories. When the "aftershocks" come rolling through, and she fears she will once again be lost in the damaging emotions, she is able to recover her balance fairly quickly. She can tell herself, "I'm *not* that scared little girl anymore; I've worked through all that, and I'm whole now." And on those days when the emotions are inevitable (anniversary dates, etc.), she can give herself permission to take a short time out to be alone and reflect on the past, knowing she will not be consumed by emotions which are out of control. In short, the abortion has finally become a closed chapter of her life, and *not the whole book.*

Sharing the Secret

After a postabortion woman has experienced healing, there is always the inevitable question: "Whom should I tell about my abortion?" After all, when you've had the emotional experience of successfully working through past pain, you want to tell the world how good it feels! If, during the course of healing, a woman comes to forgive a mother who forced the abortion decision, the natural reaction is to share that with mom. But we caution a woman to proceed very, very carefully with this decision.

The questions which must be asked before making a decision to tell someone about the abortion are: (1)What is my motive for telling this person? (2) What is the benefit of this person knowing? (3) What am I likely to get from this person? If the motive is to make the other person feel badly, if there is no benefit to this person knowing, if the person is likely to give you a negative response, then don't proceed!

Let's take the example of a mother who was heavily involved in the abortion decision, and it hasn't been discussed since it happened. This mother may feel guilty about her coerciveness, wish she could talk to her daughter about it, but not have the slightest idea how to approach the subject. On the other hand, the mother may have no regrets about the abortion decision. Only the postabortion daughter can make the best determination of her own motive for bringing it up, the probable benefit and the probable outcome. (One approach which has been quite successful is to ask the mother's forgiveness for engaging in sexual activity prior to marriage.)

The question of whether to tell one's children is always a difficult one. In our experience, young children don't have the emotional capacity for understanding the complicated reasons behind an abortion decision (although it is probably okay to say something like "mommy had a baby growing in her tummy that died before it could be born"). When telling an adolescent, permission needs to be given for a short time of anger and sadness. The adolescent needs to understand that this is a secret the mom is entrusting, and while he or she can feel free to approach mom with any questions at any time, it is mom's request that this not be discussed with anyone else because it is so private.

Be selective with whom you choose to share, and don't let a negative reaction put you in a tailspin. When you decide to tell someone about your abortion experience, *let them know ahead of time what you need from them*. Otherwise, they often simply don't know how to react.

Dealing with the Ongoing Memories

There will always be ongoing events which bring forth one or more of the painful abortion memories. You will probably always remember the anniversary of your abortion and/or the baby's original due date. Everywhere you will be confronted with prenatal pictures, baby commercials, pregnant friends, and playing children. You will never forget the child that was never born, and sometimes the pain will worse than at others. As in any grieving process, the painful days will eventually become further and further apart, and the memories less upsetting. But this may take longer than our society, with its fixation on the "instant" solutions, is usually prepared to allow any grieving person.

Be aware of the anniversary of the abortion and/or when the baby's due date would have been. *Prepare* for these days. Perhaps you need to go to a quiet, private, safe place and journal your feelings. Maybe you'll want to make arrangements to be with a close friend who knows all about the abortion and your subsequent healing process.

My two brothers were killed together on October 28, 1978. That was a long, long time ago. For years after their deaths, I would become violently sick every October 28th, never making the connection that it was an anniversary date of a very sad episode in my life. Once I finally understood that my body was remembering what I was trying to deny, I decided to start setting the day aside and take care of myself emotionally. While the intense need to do this has lessened over the years, the anniversary is still indelibly fixed in my brain.

Your baby lived, however briefly. Don't be afraid to remember and commemorate that little life.

•   •   •

Before concluding this chapter, we would like to add a postscript to Linda's story, which we told at the beginning of this book.

After two more months of depression, Linda called a Crisis Pregnancy Center located in her community. A concerned friend had told her that one of the services offered by the Center was postabortion counseling. She attended the initial session of a therapy group one night. Although the first meeting had been previously defined as primarily informational, Linda cried several times during the two-hour session.

Four sessions into therapy, Linda became a Christian through the efforts of the friend who had recommended her to the Center. Between her deepening commitment to Jesus Christ and time spent in the group, she began pulling together the pieces of her life and looking at them to figure out how she had arrived at her present situation. Her depression and late-night outbursts had decreased. When the group ended several weeks later, Linda had managed to stabilize her daily mood swings. And, finally, she was able to begin making plans for a family.

Chapter 8:
Men and Abortion

S omewhere in the constant swirl of a postabortion woman's pain is the relentless question: "Has he been hurt as much as I have?"

If you are going through your healing process right now, you might be wondering why your partner seems to be ambivalent about or even hostile toward your recovery issues. This is because every person must come to the place of healing on his or her own timetable. If you are working through the pain of your past abortion and your partner was the father of the baby, he is suddenly put in the position of being forced to look at issues perhaps before he is ready. If he was *not* the father of the baby, it is normal for him to feel threatened that you are revisiting an episode in your life that involved a sexual union with another man. Either way, men seem to approach postabortion issues with a great deal of ambivalence.

I have directed the question hundreds of times to frightened young women who have come in for a pregnancy test: "What do you think your boyfriend wants you to do if you're pregnant?" And nine times out of ten, the answer is the same: "I'm not sure what he wants. He told me he would support whatever decision I made."

This generation of men has been raised in the shadow of the feminist movement which has told them repeatedly: "A woman's body is hers, not yours. You may *not* tell her what to do with her body. You may *not* tell her what to do if she gets pregnant. She, and she alone, decides what to do with a pregnancy, and frankly, your opinion simply doesn't count. Oh, and by the way, you'll be expected to pay for the abortion."

Generally, men have followed this uncompromising commandment when it comes to their girlfriends' pregnancies. They dutifully produce the required response, "Gee, honey, it's up to you—I'll support you in whatever you decide to do." But many of these men have very strongly held convictions that abortion is wrong, and the sense of powerlessness and emasculation afterward is what leads to the breakup of so many relationships.

Arthur Shostak, a pro-choice researcher who surveyed over 1,000 men who had accompanied their wives and girlfriends to the abortion clinic, found that most of the men hid their own feelings beneath the desire to support the woman, even though 26% thought of abortion as murder. Many expressed pain and outrage that their feelings were not considered in the decision-making process. Many broke down and cried during the interview.[11]

In the frantic hurry to obtain an abortion and "deal with the problem," it is not uncommon for a couple to begin discussing their feelings *after* the abortion, when it is too late to reverse the decision. As the man begins to confess that he wishes the abortion had not happened, the woman is bewildered as to why he verbalized neutral support beforehand. It has been my experience that many women were waiting to hear their boyfriend declare, "Hey, this is *our child*—the product of our lovemaking; we'll just readjust our plans and make this happen somehow!" But because he believed he was supposed to suppress his feelings and be supportive, he remained neutral. Now the woman begins to resent his former neutrality, he becomes angry and confused as to what his role should have been, and the end of the relationship is imminent.

Men who participated in an abortion decision must go through all the healing tasks mentioned in this book. Just like a postabortion woman, he must cope with the knowledge that he overrode the powerful human instinct to protect one's own child.

The postabortion man who did *not* want the abortion is, in addition, dealing with overwhelming feelings of rage toward a system that excludes the father in an abortion decision. Furthermore, while a man is exempt from the abortion decision, he is told that he *will* support the child financially if and when the woman decides to carry to term. This double message is bewildering to men and has deeply eroded a sense of male accountability for the last two decades. A "deadbeat dad" who doesn't take financial responsibility for his offspring is considered a social misfit, while a woman's right to snuff her child's life out is held to be a constitutional right. A man who coerces a woman into having an abortion is held in the deepest contempt. But if a woman decides on an abortion against the man's wishes, no sympathy is wasted. It is not surprising that a "men's movement" has begun to sweep this nation in reaction to the emasculation men have endured under the anti-male sentiment of the radical feminist agenda.

We have become so indifferent to a man's instinctual urge to protect and provide for his children that abortion is now considered a socially acceptable outcome for a pregnancy even between two married people.

Just this week, I met with a couple who have been married several years. They both have teenagers from previous marriages, and she recently received what she thought was joyous news: they were expecting a child formed of their own union. When she shared what should have been the most sacred moment between two married people, his reaction was swift and decisive: there is no room for a baby in this family.

Rather than simply adding another plate to the family table, this child is being measured by her father in utilitarian terms only. And so far, she is coming up on the negative side of the balance sheet.

While attention has been focused on the healing needs of the postabortion woman for the past decade, little effort has been directed at the men involved in the abortion decision. But Crisis Pregnancy Centers are getting more and more calls from postabortion men asking for help, and men's support groups are now beginning to appear across the country.

I will never forget the night I was privileged to listen to a small group of men who had been meeting together and going through *Women in Ramah*[22]. While grateful for any tool at all, they poignantly expressed the additional issues confronting the men of abortion. They talked about the loss of fatherhood and what it meant to them. They began describing their deep and utter feelings of failure before God to be protectors. They were still in the process of healing and I could sense the depth of their woundedness.

From that evening was born a new workbook, *Turning A Father's Heart*[33], which is now being widely used to help men who are hungry for healing. If you or someone you know needs this kind of healing from the pain of lost fatherhood, I would urge you to write to one of the organizations listed in the back of this book. Or call a local Crisis Pregnancy Center and ask for help.

---

1. Arthur Shostak and Gary McLouth with Lynn Seng. *Men and Abortion*. New York: Praeger Publishers, 1984.

2. *Women in Ramah*, by Linda Cochrane, is the most widely used postabortion Bible study in this country. See the bibliography for ordering information.

3 *Turning A Father's Heart*, by Linda Cochrane and Kathy Jones. See bibliography for ordering information.

Bibliography

* = recommended reading for those hurting from a past abortion

*BAKER, DON, *Beyond Choice: The Abortion Story No One Is Telling*. Portland, Oregon: Multnomah Press, 1985. (This short book is the true, straight-forward account of one woman's abortion experiences, and how profoundly they continue to affect her. Unhelpful in that only a couple of pages at the very end attempt to deal with any healing Debbie sustained. Extremely helpful in that it carefully and agonizingly documents the pain a post-abortion woman suffers.)

*COCHRANE, LINDA and JONES, LINDA, *Turning a Father's Heart*. For ordering information, write to Linda Cochrane, Rte. 164 Box 232, Patterson, NY 12563. (This first workbook for men, published in 1994, is a wonderful study for men only.)

*COCHRANE, LINDA, *Women in Ramah: A Post-Abortion Bible Study*. For ordering information, write to Linda Cochrane, Rte. 164 Box 232, Patterson, NY 12563. (This is the best workbook for use in groups that we've come across so far. The chapters cover all the task areas mentioned in this volume.)

COLLINS, GARY R., *Can You Trust Psychology?* Downers Grove, Illinois: InterVarsity Press, 1988. (The author has done an admirable job delineating the growing hostility—in some quarters—between theology and psychology, and completely defuses the debate by demonstrating that the two arenas are completely compatible. Required reading for any lay counselor operating in an environment where the word "psychology" is anathema.)

*ERVIN, PAULA, *Women Exploited: The Other Victims of Abortion*. Huntington, IN: Our Sunday Visitor, Inc., 1985. (A poignant collection of case histories from women who have come through WEBA groups. Lists WEBA and Right To Life chapters around the country.)

*FREED, LUCY and SALAZER, PENNY, *A Season For Healing*. Thomas Nelson Publishers, 1993. (A wonderful new tool—especially for those who might be threatened by the overt spiritual approach of other workbooks.)

*KOERBEL, PAM, *Abortion's Second Victim*. Wheaton, IL: Victor Books, 1986. (This volume includes the author's own personal account of her abortion experience and subsequent healing, a helpful section on what motivates women to abort, and a moving explanation of how to accept God's forgiveness.)

*KOERBEL, PAM, *Does Anyone Else Feel Like I Do?* New York, NY: Bantam Doubleday Dell Publishing Group, Inc., 1990. (This helpful book is unique in that it is written in a question and answer format.)

MALL, DAVID AND WATTS, WALTER F., *The Psychological Aspects of Abortion*. Washington, D.C.: University Publications of America, 1979. (Although dated at this point, this book retains an important place on the bookshelf of those who want to know about the earlier studies investigating the existence of PAS.)

*MANNION, MICHAEL T., *Abortion and Healing: A Cry To Be Whole*. Kansas City, Missouri: Sheed and Ward, 1986. (Another excellent resource for the woman who hurts from a past abortion. Father Mannion has been a pioneer in this field.)

*MC CLUNG, JR., FLOYD, *The Father Heart of God*. Eugene, Oregon: Harvest House Publishers, 1985.

(The importance of this book cannot be overestimated in working particularly with women who have a Christian worldview. This elegantly-written volume does a magnificent job of correcting the reader's misperceptions of a judgmental God and replacing it with an approachable image of God as a loving father.)

*MICHELS, NANCY, *Helping Women Recover From Abortion*. Minneapolis, MN: Bethany House Publishers, 1988. (This excellent book includes, among other topics, an commendable explanation of the grieving process through which the post-abortion woman proceeds. Also contains a much needed chapter on how abortion affects others involved in the abortion decision.)

MINIRTH, FRANK B., AND MEIER, PAUL D., *Happiness Is A Choice*. Grand Rapids, Michigan: Baker Book House Co., 1978. (This manual describing the symptoms, causes, and cures of depression, is the best of its kind, in our opinion. Drs. Minirth and Meier have written in a style easily understood by anyone, and is a basic tool for anyone dealing with depression.)

NOUWEN, HENRI J. M., *The Wounded Healer*. Garden City, New York: Image Books, 1979. (Although not specifically written on the subject of post-abortion trauma, this tiny book is required reading for anyone attempting to deal with the emotional suffering of another human being. We cannot praise this little monograph highly enough as a basic primer for all would-be counselors!)

Our Healing Journey, Diocese of Lansing, Project Rachel, 1500 E. Saginaw St., Lansing, MI 48906. (A post-abortion study especially good for women of Catholic backgrounds.)

*PERETTI, FRANK E., *Tilly*. Westchester, Illinois: Crossway Books, 1988. (This short novel describes "Kathy's" dream/vision as she meets the child she aborted years ago. It is extremely touching and powerful in helping a post-abortion woman grieve for the loss of her aborted baby. There is much hope built in to the story.)

*Post Abortion Supprt Group Manual, Heartbeat International, 1213 1/2 S. James Rd., Columbus, Ohio 43227 (614) 239-9433. (Heartbeat, International is a fairly new pro-life organization with a growing number of crisis pregnancy centers.)

REARDON, DAVID, *Abortion Women: Silent No More.* Chicago, Illinois: Loyola University Press, 1987. (Dr. Reardon discusses the results of a survey administered to post-abortion women through WEBA chapters in many different states. In addition, there are several well-written chapters with such provocative titles as "Feminists Who Abort," "The Impact of Abortion on Later Children," and "Before and After Legalization." Excellent case studies described to illustrate his points.

REISSER, TERI, *Guidelines for Leading a Post-Abortion Support Group.* CareNet, 101 W. Broad St., #500, Falls Church, VA 22046.

*SELBY, TERRY and BOCKMON, MARC, *The Mourning After: Help for Postabortion Syndrome.* Grand Rapids, Michigan: Baker Book House, 1990.

SHOSTAK, ARTHUR AND MCLOUTH, GARY, *Men and Abortion.* New York: Praeger Publishers, 1984. (Dr. Shostak surveyed 1,000 men as they waited for their partners to get abortions. In addition, 75 post-abortion men were interviewed about the aftermath of their abortion experiences. This book rocked the pro-life camp because Dr. Shostak, a strong pro-choice advocate, reported that a strong majority of the men he surveyed were having problems with the abortion. However, the book operates wholly on the premise that if men—and, presumably, women—were only given better pre-abortion counseling, most of these problems could be eliminated. A valuable tool for those hoping to work with postabortion victims; just be aware of the strong pro-choice ideology.)

SPECKHARD, ANNE, *Psycho-social Stress Following Abortion*. Kansas City, MO: Sheed & Ward, 1987. (Dr. Speckhard's significant study of how abortion affects behavior is described and summarized.)

*STANFORD, SUSAN M., *Will I Cry Tomorrow?* Old Tappan, New Jersey: Fleming Revell Co., 1986. (The author's own experience with an abortion and subsequent post-abortion trauma. Beautifully written from a Catholic framework, Dr. Stanford elegantly describes the inner healing she finally experienced, and outlines healing steps for the reader.)

*VOUGHT, JEANETTE, *Post-Abortion Trauma: 9 Steps To Recovery*. Grand Rapids, Michigan: Zondervan Publishing House, 1991. (A recovery plan based on the Conquerors Program.)

*WINKLER, KATHLEEN, *When the Crying Stops: Abortion, The Pain and the Healing*. Milwaukee, Wisconsin: Northwestern Publishing House, 1991.

Where to Find Help

*Good source of information regarding PAS
**Will provide information as well as counseling for PAS
***Will provide information and counseling for PAS as well as training for those who want to become postabortion counselors.

ABORTION TRAUMA SERVICES
AND OUTREACH**
1608 13th Ave. S. #112
Birmingham, AL 35202
(Associated with Sav-A-Life)

AMERICAN RIGHTS COALITION
PO Box 487
Chattanooga, TN 37401
(800) 634-2224
(Hotline for post abortion medical,
emotional and legal complications)

AMERICAN VICTIMS OF ABORTION*
Olivia Gans, Director
419 7th St., NW Suite 402
Washington, DC 20004
(202) 626-8800

ASSOCIATION FOR INTERDISCIPLINARY
RESEARCH IN VALUES AND
SOCIAL CHANGE*
419 7th Street NW #500
Washington, DC 20004
(202) 626-8800
(An organization made up of pro-life professionals
and researchers; newsletter is excellent.)

CARENET***(formerly Christian Action Council)
101 W. Broad St., #500
Falls Church, VA 22046
(703) 237-2100
(A source for "Women in Ramah"
(800) 237-5030 for orders only)

LINDA COCHRANE*
Rte. 164, Box 232
Patterson, NY 12563
(914) 878-7789
(Source of Women in Ramah and
Turning a Father's Heart)

ELLIOT INSTITUTE
PO Box 9079
Springfield, IL 62791-9079
(Publishes an excellent quarterly newsletter
"Post Abortion Review", edited by David Reardon,
$20.00 annually. Sample $1.00)

HEALING VISIONS NETWORK*
National Youth Pro-Life Coalition
Jackson Avenue
Hastings on Hudson, NY 10706
(Source of excellent tapes from their annual Healing
Visions Conferences.)

HEARTBEAT, INTERNATIONAL**
1213 1/2 S. James Road
Columbus, OH 43227
(614) 239-9433

HUMAN LIFE INTERNATIONAL*
7845-E Airpark Rd.
Gaithersburg, MD 20879
(301) 670-7884
(800) 549-5433

NATIONAL OFFICE OF POST ABORTION
RECONCILIATION AND HEALING
PO Box 07477
Milwaukee, WI 53207-0477
(414) 483-4141
(800) 593-2273

POST ABORTION MINISTRIES, INC.
PO Box 3092
Landover Hills, MD 20784-0092
(301) 773-4630

PROJECT RACHEL**
Diocese of Lansing
1500 E. Saginaw St.
Lansing, MI 48906.
(Publishes *Our Healing Journey*, a post-abortion study
especially good for women of Catholic backgrounds.)

TERI REISSER***
Right To Life League of Southern California
1028 N. Lake Ave. #102
Pasadena, CA 91104
(818) 398-6100

DR. VINCENT RUE**
DR. ANNE SPECKHARD
DR. SUSAN STANFORD RUE
Institute for Abortion Recovery and Research
111 Bow Street
Portsmouth, NH 03801
(603) 431-1904

TERRY SELBY, M.S.W.**
Counseling Associates of Bemidji
P.O. Box 577
Bemidji, MN 56601
(218) 751-9510
(An in-patient setting for treatment of PAS.)

IN CANADA:
STRAIGHT TALK
1669 Bayview Ave., Ste 203
Toronto, ON M4G 3C1
(416) 485-9773

IN THE UNITED KINGDOM:
BRITISH VICTIMS OF ABORTION**
S.P.U.C.
7 Tufton Street
London, SW1P 3QN
England

Order Form

Price list for Help for the Post Abortion Woman

Single copy $8.95 (postpaid)

2 to 9 copies	$5.95 each
10 to 24 copies	$5.50 each
25 to 49 copies	$4.95 each
50 to 99 copies	$4.50 each
100 or more	$3.95 each

(for orders of 2 or more books please add 10% shipping & handling, with a minimum charge of $3.95)

Order from:

LIFE CYCLE BOOKS,

PO BOX 420, Lewiston, NY 14092-0420

Phone: (416) 690-5860   Fax: (416) 690-8532

- -

Please send me _____ copy(ies) of HELP FOR THE POST ABORTION WOMAN.

Enclosed please find $ _____ to cover the cost of books and shipping.

Send book(s) to:

Name: _____

Address: _____

State: _____

Zip Code: _____

Order Form

Price list for Help for the Post Abortion Woman

Single copy $8.95 (postpaid)

2 to 9 copies	$5.95 each
10 to 24 copies	$5.50 each
25 to 49 copies	$4.95 each
50 to 99 copies	$4.50 each
100 or more	$3.95 each

(for orders of 2 or more books please add 10% shipping & handling, with a minimum charge of $3.95)

Order from:
LIFE CYCLE BOOKS,
PO BOX 420, Lewiston, NY 14092-0420
Phone: (416) 690-5860   Fax: (416) 690-8532

- -

Please send me _____ copy(ies) of HELP FOR THE POST ABORTION WOMAN.

Enclosed please find $ _____ to cover the cost of books and shipping.

Send book(s) to:

Name: _____

Address: _____

State: _____

Zip Code: _____